Praise for *Maroon Comix*

"I was drawn immediately into this exceptionally stimulating world of history and I didn't put *Maroon Comix* down until the very last page! It was as if I too was in the swamplands and running through the forests and up into the hills, determined to live Free! I love how the circularly positioned routes of art and text take one on an in depth journey into realms of resistance that many have never known existed! *This* is how history should be taught! I am inspired . . . I am elevated . . . and I too am Maroon!"
—Mama Charlotte Hill O'Neal aka Iya Osotunde Fasuyi, Black Panther Party, Kansas City Chapter, cofounder of the United African Alliance Community Center, Tanzania

"*Maroon Comix* is breathtaking! I say that after decades of study and practice in that arena. One who is serious about resisting the dragons that threaten our very existence, will use *Maroon Comix* to help fashion or reinforce their place within the hydra of twenty-first-century maroons."
—Russell Maroon Shoatz, political prisoner and author of *Maroon the Implacable*

"The history and stories that the maroons personified should inspire a whole new generation of abolitionists. This comic can motivate all those looking to resist modern capitalism's twenty-first-century slavery and the neofascism we are facing today."
—Dhoruba Bin Wahad, Black Panther Party, New York Chapter, executive director of Community Change Africa

"One of the best things in the history of the world."
—John P. Clark, author of *The Impossible Community*, founder of La Terre Institute for Community and Ecology

"Marronage—the art of being a maroon—needs to be expanded into a principle of resistance to the totality and the construction of a new reality: the Great Dismal Swamp as living utopia. This fine comic book ('comic' because it's not 'tragic') should be infiltrated into every schoolhouse and factory in 'Capitalist Modernity'!"
—Hakim Bey, author of *TAZ: The Temporary Autonomous Zone*

"With bold graphics and urgent prose, *Maroon Comix* provides a powerful antidote to toxic historical narratives. By showing us what was, Quincy Saul and his talented team allow us to see what's possible."
—James Sturm, author of *The Golem's Mighty Swing* and *Market Day*, cofounder of the Center for Cartoon Studies

"The activist artists of *Maroon Comix* have combined and presented struggles past and present in a vivid, creative graphic form, pointing a way toward an emancipated future."
—Marcus Rediker, coauthor of *The Many-Headed Hydra* and author of *The Slave Ship: A Human History*

"Quincy Saul is an imaginative agitpropper. Influenced by Fred Ho, Russell Maroon Shoatz, and god knows who else, he is a creative force to be reckoned with. I think he underestimates the value of state power and the struggle to control the state but his ability to use counter-hegemonic concepts and turn them into revolutionary images is very advanced. I love reading/watching/learning/ disagreeing with/appreciating his work."
—Eric Mann, founder of the Labor Community Strategy Center, author of *Playbook for Progressives* and *Comrade George*

"I very much enjoyed *Maroon Comix*—quite an artistically lively and politically vital project. It provides a graphically vivid and easily readable account of the history that the ruling class has done all in its power to bury. And, very importantly, this work presents ways to build on and carry forward today the wonderfully liberatory spirit of the maroons."
—David Gilbert, political prisoner and author of *Love and Struggle*

"*Maroon Comix*, a marvelously scripted and drawn comic, will bring a new generation of readers information and insights into the brave struggle of slaves and their supporters to create free communities of color."
—Paul Buhle, retired lecturer, Brown University, editor of *Red Rosa*, *Che*, *A People's History of American Empire*, and other comics

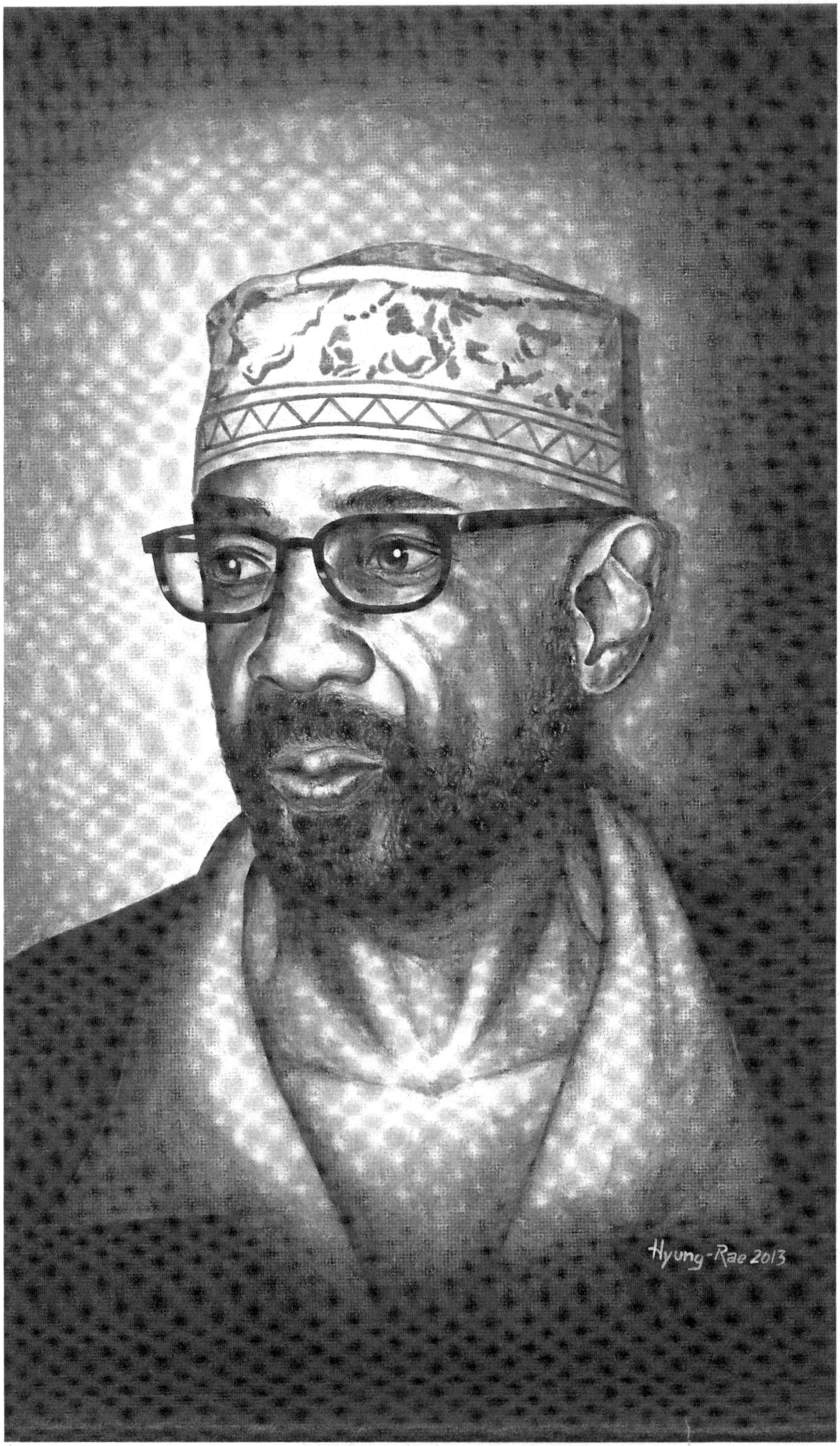
Hyung-Rae 2013

Portrait of Russell Maroon Shoatz by Todd Hyung-Rae Tarselli

MAROON COMIX

Origins and Destinies

Conceived, compiled, and coordinated by

Quincy Saul

Illustrated by

Songe Riddle, Mac McGill, Seth Tobocman,
Hannah Allen, Emmy Kepler, and Mikaela González

With selections primarily from the writings of Russell Maroon Shoatz,
and citations from Gaanman Joachim-Joseph Adochini, James Koehnline,
Herbert Aptheker, Mavis Campbell, Wade Davis, Dan Hancox, C.L.R.
James, Sabu Kohso, Butch Lee, Julius Nyerere, Abdullah Öcalan,
Richard Price, Juan Manuel Sánchez Gordillo, and more . . .

PM PRESS

ECOSOCIALIST HORIZONS

Dedicated to Fred Ho

Thanks to: Russell Maroon Shoatz, Fred Ho, Ann Greene, Frances Lu Houn, Flora Hoffman and Florence Houn, Melanie West, Lutie Spitzer, Kanya D'Almeida, Matt Meyer, Steven DeCastro, John P. Clark, Eric Tenza, Joel Kovel, Cesar Escalona, Richard Price, spiritchild, Ben Barson . . . and to all the maroons in the Dazzling Swamp, all the compas in the East Coast Chiapas Solidarity Committee, all the cadre in a new black arts movement, and all fellow travelers toward ecosocialist horizons . . .

Half of all royalties from sales of this book will be donated to the Musa Henderson Memorial Fund, established to aid selected individuals and organizations who work on behalf of achieving human rights for the oppressed from all backgrounds.

Maroon Comix: Origins and Destinies
Edited by Quincy Saul

This edition © PM Press 2018

Front cover illustration by Mikaela González
Layout by Jonathan Rowland

PM Press
PO Box 23912
Oakland, CA 94623
www.pmpress.org

Questions? Answers? Contact us at
prefiguration@gmail.com / www.ecosocialisthorizons.com

ISBN: 978-1-62963-571-2
Library of Congress Control Number: 2018931521

10 9 8 7 6 5 4 3 2 1

Printed in the USA

Contents

Initiation

illustrated by Songe Riddle

When you live IN the map you hardly notice these things

any more than you notice the nameless ones silently slipping beyond the pale, leaving the map behind.

Who cares who goes there, who goes nowhere?"

"LEGEND OF THE GREAT DISMAL MAROONS", BY JAMES KOEHNLINE (GONE TO CROATAN P79-87)

YOU ARE INVITED HERE TO A JOURNEY OFF THE MAP.

THESE ARE THE HISTORIES AND PROPHECIES OF **MAROONS**, WHO FOR CENTURIES BUILT SOCIETIES AND NETWORKS OF LIBERATION AROUND THE WORLD.

ever since 1524 when the Spanish founded the first European (and African) settlement in what is now the U.S.,

slaves had been walking away from bondage, joining or forging alliances with friendly Indian nations."

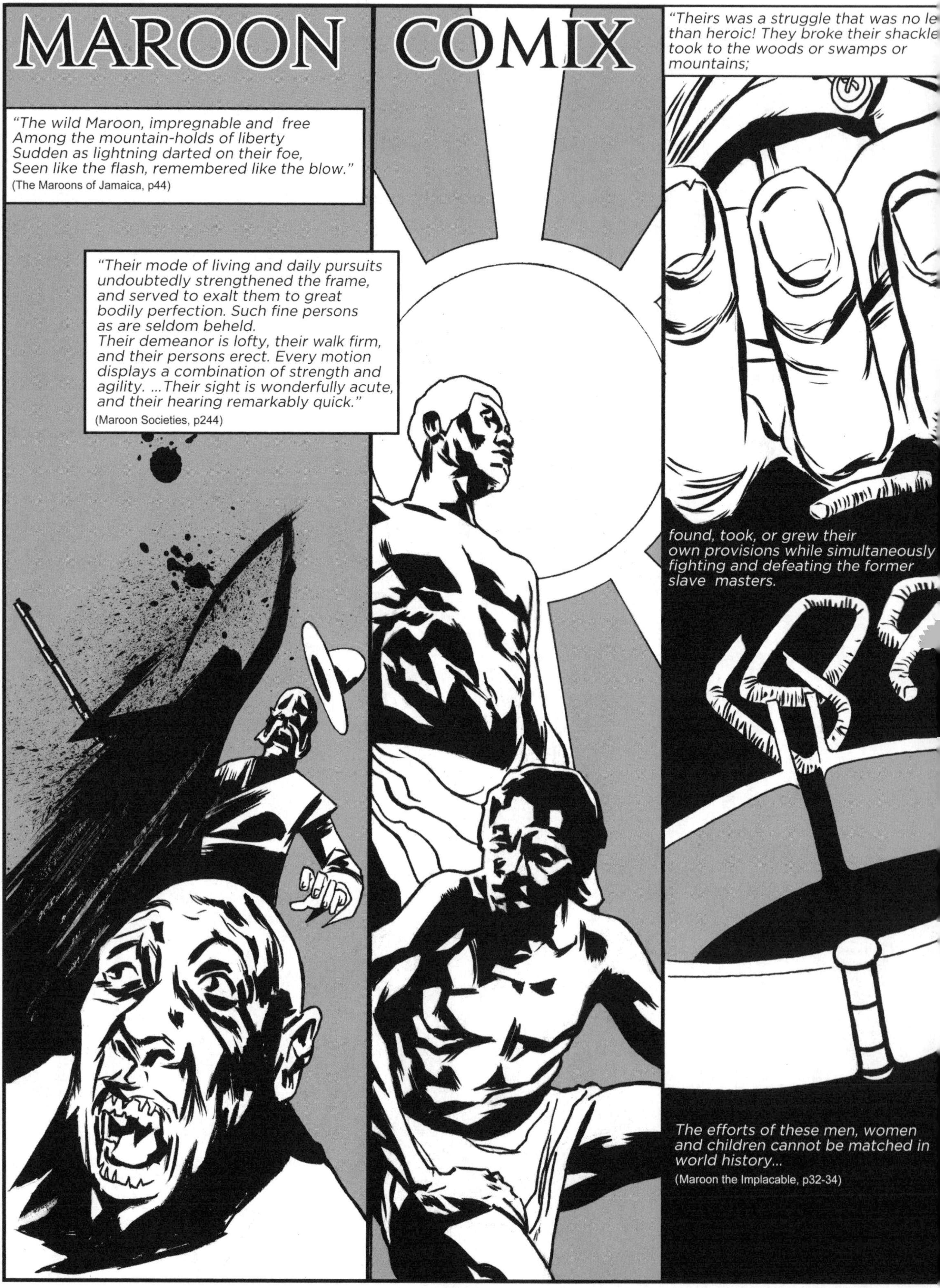
MAROON COMIX
"The wild Maroon, impregnable and free
Among the mountain-holds of liberty
Sudden as lightning darted on their foe,
Seen like the flash, remembered like the blow."
(The Maroons of Jamaica, p44)
"Their mode of living and daily pursuits undoubtedly strengthened the frame, and served to exalt them to great bodily perfection. Such fine persons as are seldom beheld.
Their demeanor is lofty, their walk firm, and their persons erect. Every motion displays a combination of strength and agility. ...Their sight is wonderfully acute, and their hearing remarkably quick."
(Maroon Societies, p244)
"Theirs was a struggle that was no le
than heroic! They broke their shackle
took to the woods or swamps or mountains;
found, took, or grew their own provisions while simultaneously fighting and defeating the former slave masters.
The efforts of these men, women and children cannot be matched in world history...
(Maroon the Implacable, p32-34)

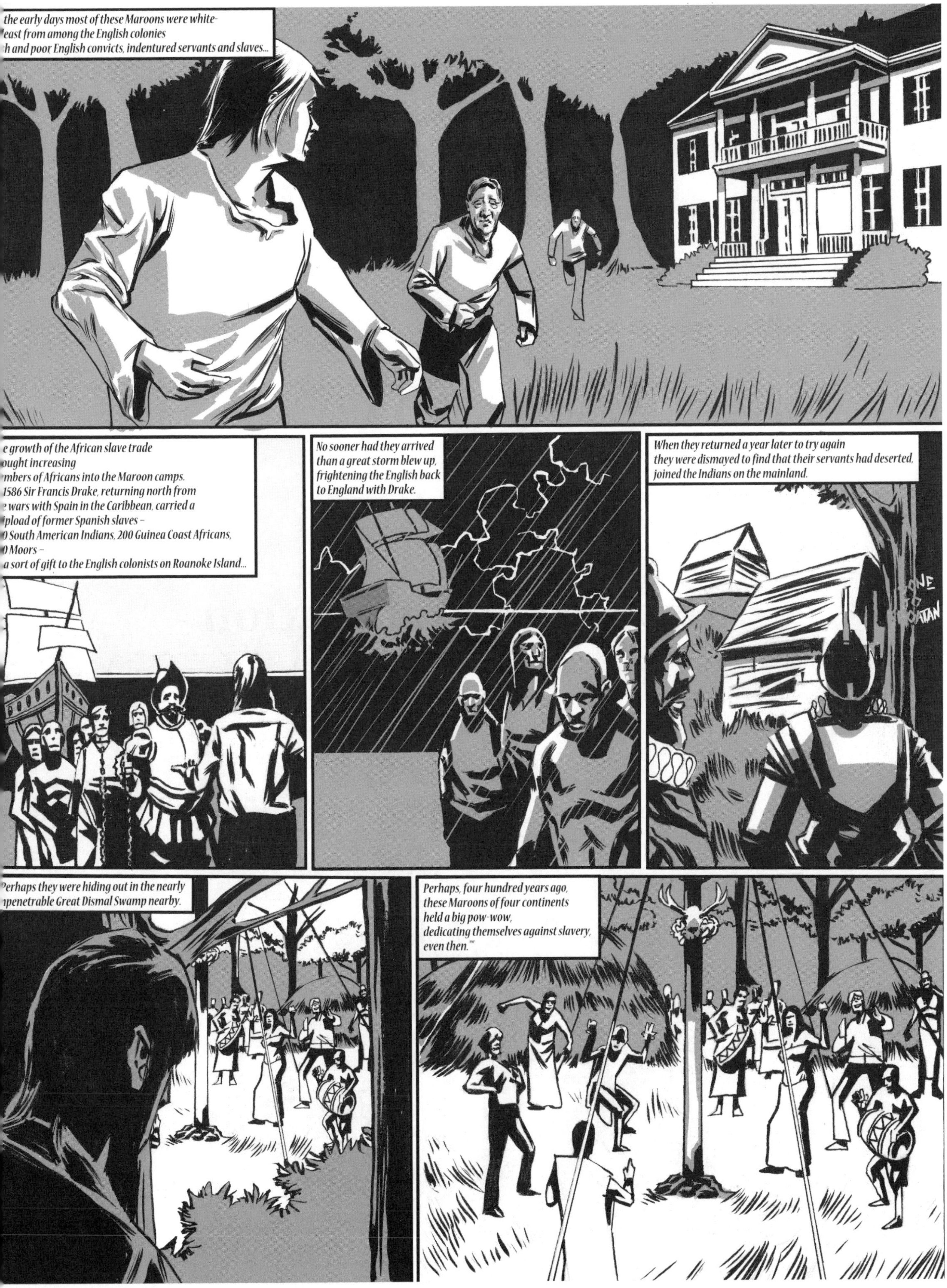
the early days most of these Maroons were white-
east from among the English colonies
h and poor English convicts, indentured servants and slaves...
e growth of the African slave trade
ought increasing
mbers of Africans into the Maroon camps.
1586 Sir Francis Drake, returning north from
wars with Spain in the Caribbean, carried a
pload of former Spanish slaves –
0 South American Indians, 200 Guinea Coast Africans,
0 Moors –
a sort of gift to the English colonists on Roanoke Island...
No sooner had they arrived
than a great storm blew up,
frightening the English back
to England with Drake.
When they returned a year later to try again
they were dismayed to find that their servants had deserted,
joined the Indians on the mainland.
Perhaps they were hiding out in the nearly
penetrable Great Dismal Swamp nearby.
Perhaps, four hundred years ago,
these Maroons of four continents
held a big pow-wow,
dedicating themselves against slavery,
even then."

Slavery and Liberation

illustrated by Songe Riddle

THE STORY OF SLAVERY

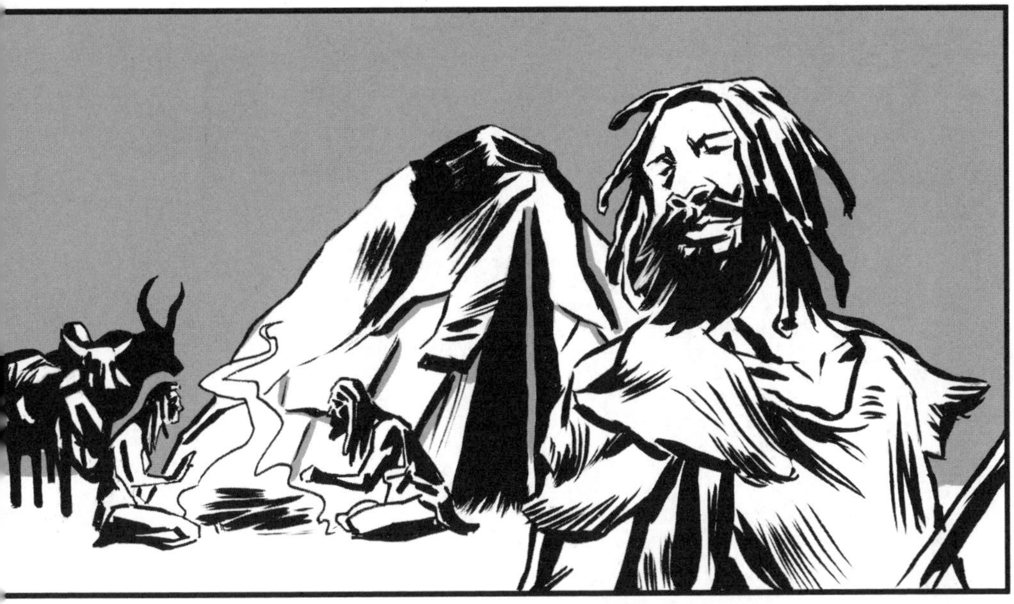

SOME SAY SLAVERY IS AS OLD AS TIME. BUT IN FACT SLAVERY IS RELATIVELY RECENT.

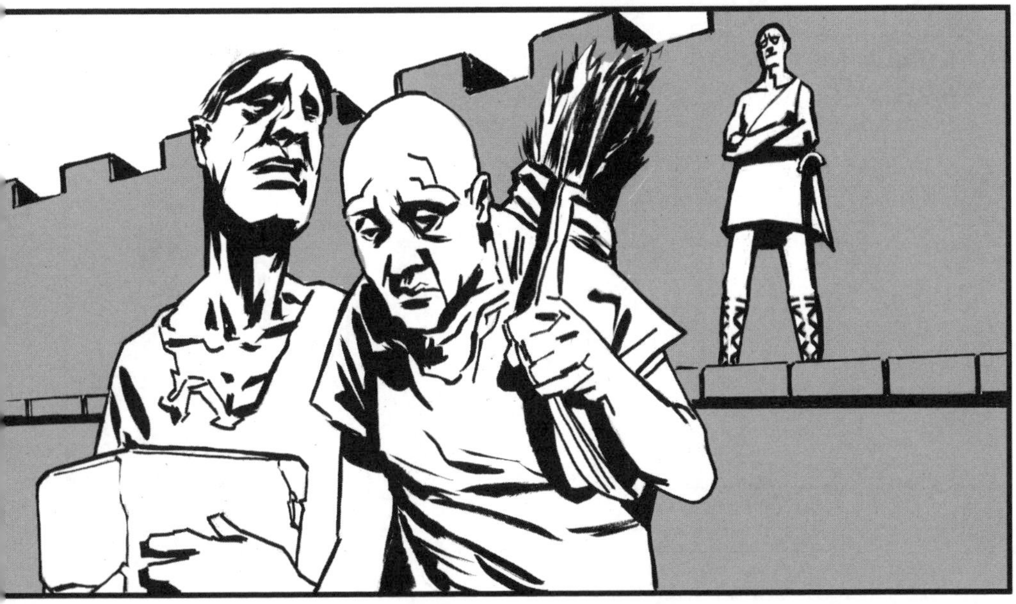

HUMANITY HAS LIVED IN FREEDOM AND RELATIVE HARMONY FOR THE VAST MAJORITY OF OUR TIME ON EARTH. SLAVERY BEGAN TO APPEAR ONLY IN THE LAST 6,000 YEARS.

BUT IN THE WHOLE HORROR STORY OF SLAVERY, NOTHING COMPARES TO THE TRANSATLANTIC SLAVE TRADE, PERHAPS THE MOST HIDEOUS CHAPTER IN HUMAN HISTORY.

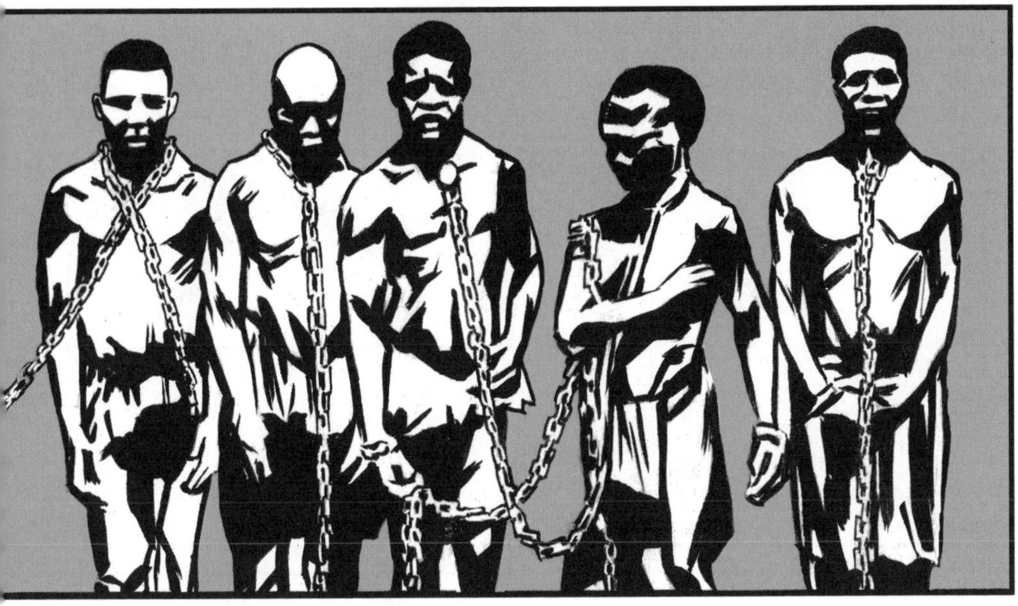

FROM ABOUT 1500 TO 1850, EUROPEAN KINGS, CHURCHES, MERCHANTS, SOLDIERS, AND SAILORS TOOK MILLIONS OF CAPTIVES FROM ALL OVER AFRICA, SHIPPED THEM ACROSS THE OCEAN, AND USED AND ABUSED THEM AS WORKERS IN THE COLONIES.

MILLIONS DIED ON THE SLAVE SHIPS, AND THE MILLIONS WHO SURVIVED FACED A LIVING HELL.

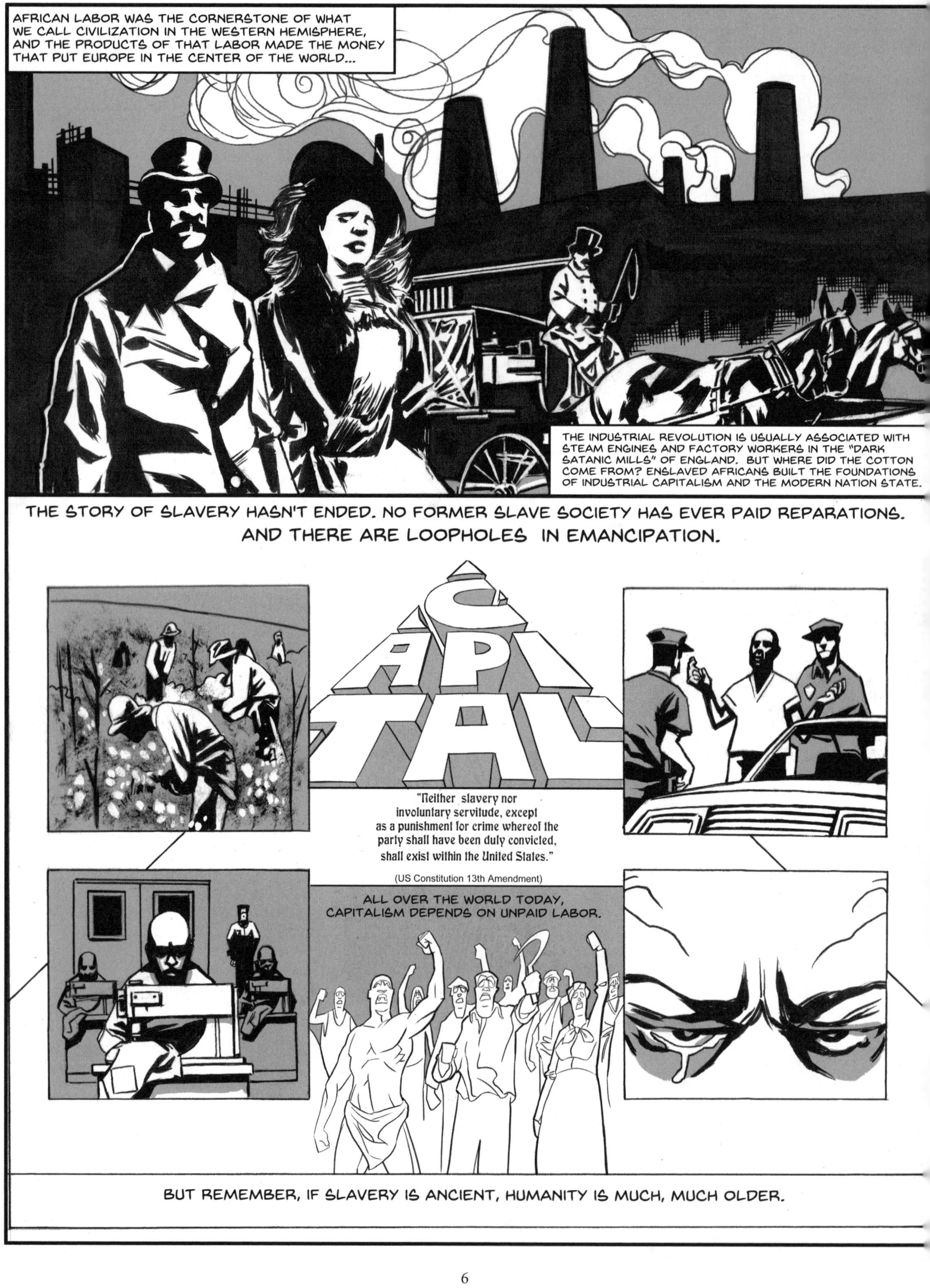
AFRICAN LABOR WAS THE CORNERSTONE OF WHAT WE CALL CIVILIZATION IN THE WESTERN HEMISPHERE, AND THE PRODUCTS OF THAT LABOR MADE THE MONEY THAT PUT EUROPE IN THE CENTER OF THE WORLD...
THE INDUSTRIAL REVOLUTION IS USUALLY ASSOCIATED WITH STEAM ENGINES AND FACTORY WORKERS IN THE "DARK SATANIC MILLS" OF ENGLAND. BUT WHERE DID THE COTTON COME FROM? ENSLAVED AFRICANS BUILT THE FOUNDATIONS OF INDUSTRIAL CAPITALISM AND THE MODERN NATION STATE.
THE STORY OF SLAVERY HASN'T ENDED. NO FORMER SLAVE SOCIETY HAS EVER PAID REPARATIONS. AND THERE ARE LOOPHOLES IN EMANCIPATION.
CAPITAL
"Neither slavery nor involuntary servitude, except as a punishment for crime whereof the party shall have been duly convicted, shall exist within the United States."
(US Constitution 13th Amendment)
ALL OVER THE WORLD TODAY, CAPITALISM DEPENDS ON UNPAID LABOR.
BUT REMEMBER, IF SLAVERY IS ANCIENT, HUMANITY IS MUCH, MUCH OLDER.

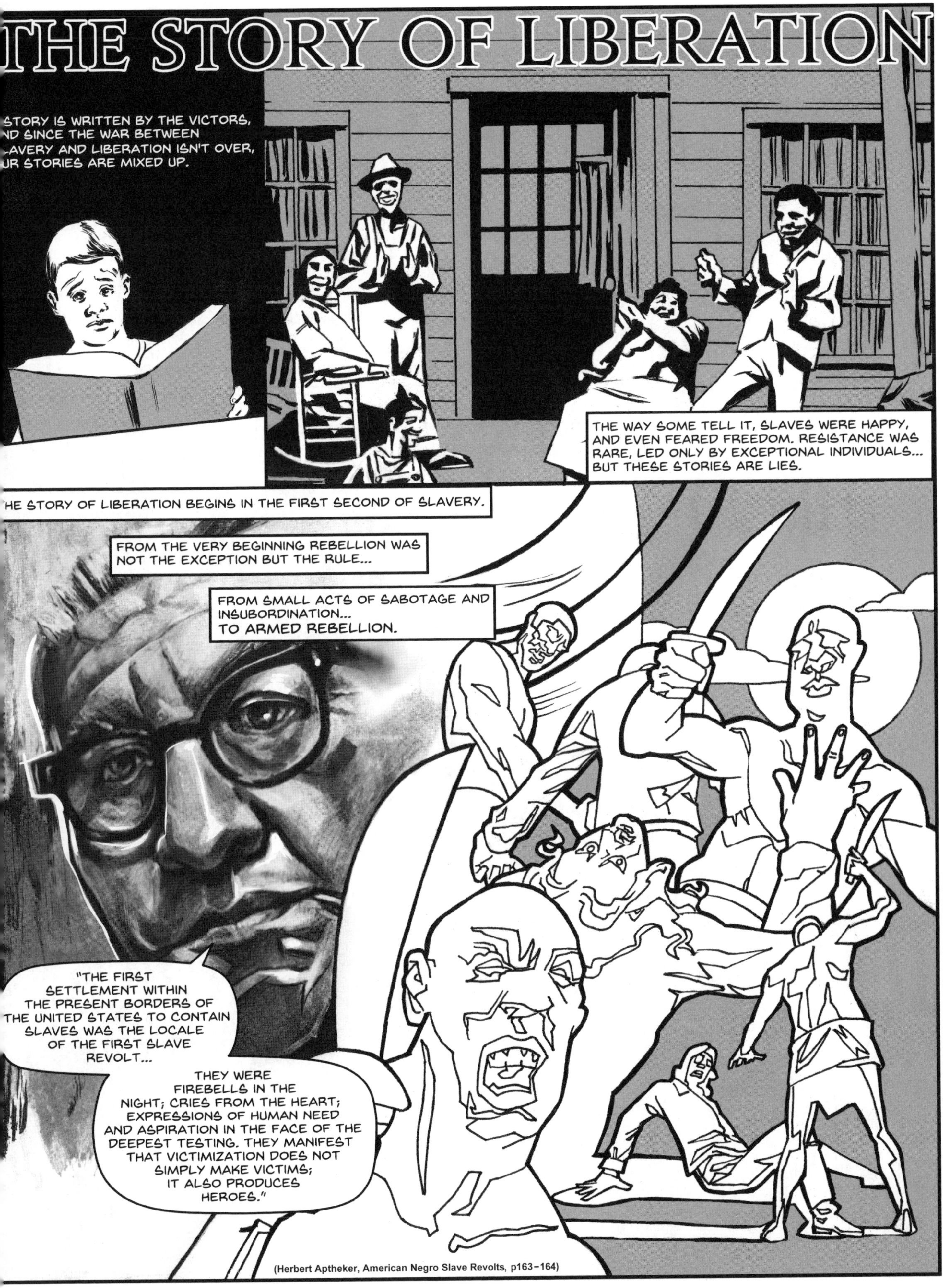

THE STORY OF LIBERATION
STORY IS WRITTEN BY THE VICTORS, ND SINCE THE WAR BETWEEN LAVERY AND LIBERATION ISN'T OVER, UR STORIES ARE MIXED UP.
THE WAY SOME TELL IT, SLAVES WERE HAPPY, AND EVEN FEARED FREEDOM. RESISTANCE WAS RARE, LED ONLY BY EXCEPTIONAL INDIVIDUALS... BUT THESE STORIES ARE LIES.
HE STORY OF LIBERATION BEGINS IN THE FIRST SECOND OF SLAVERY.
FROM THE VERY BEGINNING REBELLION WAS NOT THE EXCEPTION BUT THE RULE...
FROM SMALL ACTS OF SABOTAGE AND INSUBORDINATION... TO ARMED REBELLION.
"THE FIRST SETTLEMENT WITHIN THE PRESENT BORDERS OF THE UNITED STATES TO CONTAIN SLAVES WAS THE LOCALE OF THE FIRST SLAVE REVOLT...
THEY WERE FIREBELLS IN THE NIGHT; CRIES FROM THE HEART; EXPRESSIONS OF HUMAN NEED AND ASPIRATION IN THE FACE OF THE DEEPEST TESTING. THEY MANIFEST THAT VICTIMIZATION DOES NOT SIMPLY MAKE VICTIMS; IT ALSO PRODUCES HEROES."
(Herbert Aptheker, American Negro Slave Revolts, p163–164)

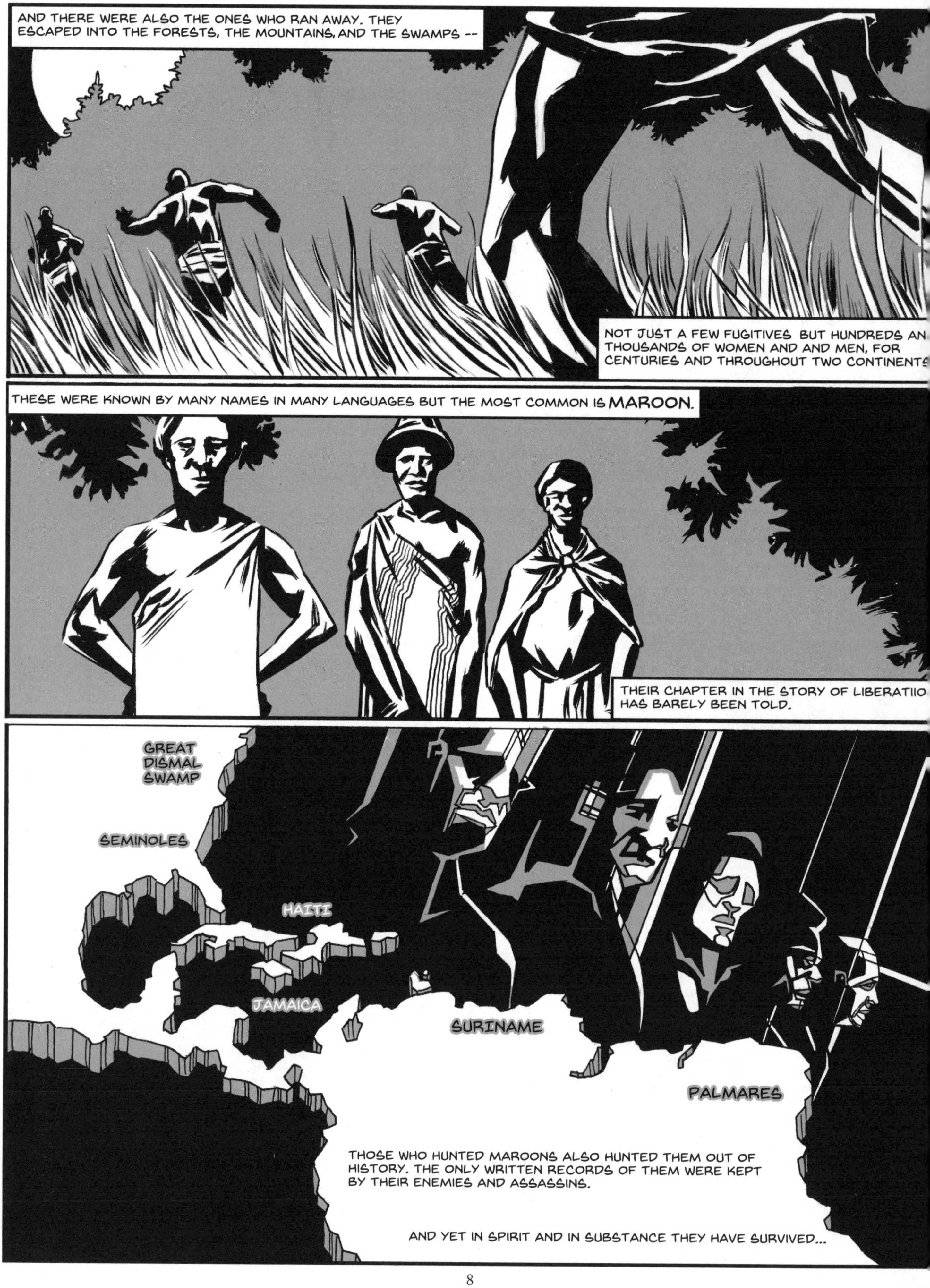
AND THERE WERE ALSO THE ONES WHO RAN AWAY. THEY ESCAPED INTO THE FORESTS, THE MOUNTAINS, AND THE SWAMPS --
NOT JUST A FEW FUGITIVES BUT HUNDREDS AN THOUSANDS OF WOMEN AND AND MEN, FOR CENTURIES AND THROUGHOUT TWO CONTINENTS
THESE WERE KNOWN BY MANY NAMES IN MANY LANGUAGES BUT THE MOST COMMON IS MAROON.
THEIR CHAPTER IN THE STORY OF LIBERATIO HAS BARELY BEEN TOLD.
GREAT DISMAL SWAMP
SEMINOLES
HAITI
JAMAICA
SURINAME
PALMARES
THOSE WHO HUNTED MAROONS ALSO HUNTED THEM OUT OF HISTORY. THE ONLY WRITTEN RECORDS OF THEM WERE KEPT BY THEIR ENEMIES AND ASSASSINS.
AND YET IN SPIRIT AND IN SUBSTANCE THEY HAVE SURVIVED...

IN JAMAICA TWO POWERFUL GROUPS OF MAROONS CONTROLLED LARGE PARTS OF THE ISLAND FOR OVER A HUNDRED YEARS, DEFEATING THE BRITISH IN MANY BATTLES.

THE JAMAICAN MAROONS HAD EXTENSIVE TRADE WITH OTHER ISLANDS AND WORKED TOGETHER WITH EUROPEAN RENEGADES.

"FOR THREE CENTURIES, BEGINNING IN THE EARLY 1500S, THERE WERE MAROONS WHO FOUGHT ALONGSIDE PIRATES IN THEIR NAVAL BATTLES, GUIDED THEM IN THEIR RAIDS ON MAJOR CITIES, AND PARTICIPATED WITH THEM IN WIDESPREAD, ILLICIT INTERNATIONAL TRADE."

(Maroon Societies, p14)

"THE PIRATES HAVE NOW BECOME A FEARED NATION, EVEN IF THEY HAVE NOT YET BEEN RECOGNIZED BY ANY GOVERNMENT."

(Maroon Societies, p55)

THE DESCENDANTS OF THESE REMAINING MAROON COMMUNITIES IN JAMAICA STILL CONTINUE TO OCCUPY THE LANDS THEY FOUGHT ON...

AND THEY'VE NEVER RECOGNIZED ANY OVERLORDS, NEITHER THE LATER BRITISH NOR BLACK GOVERNMENT"
(Maroon the Implacable, p115)

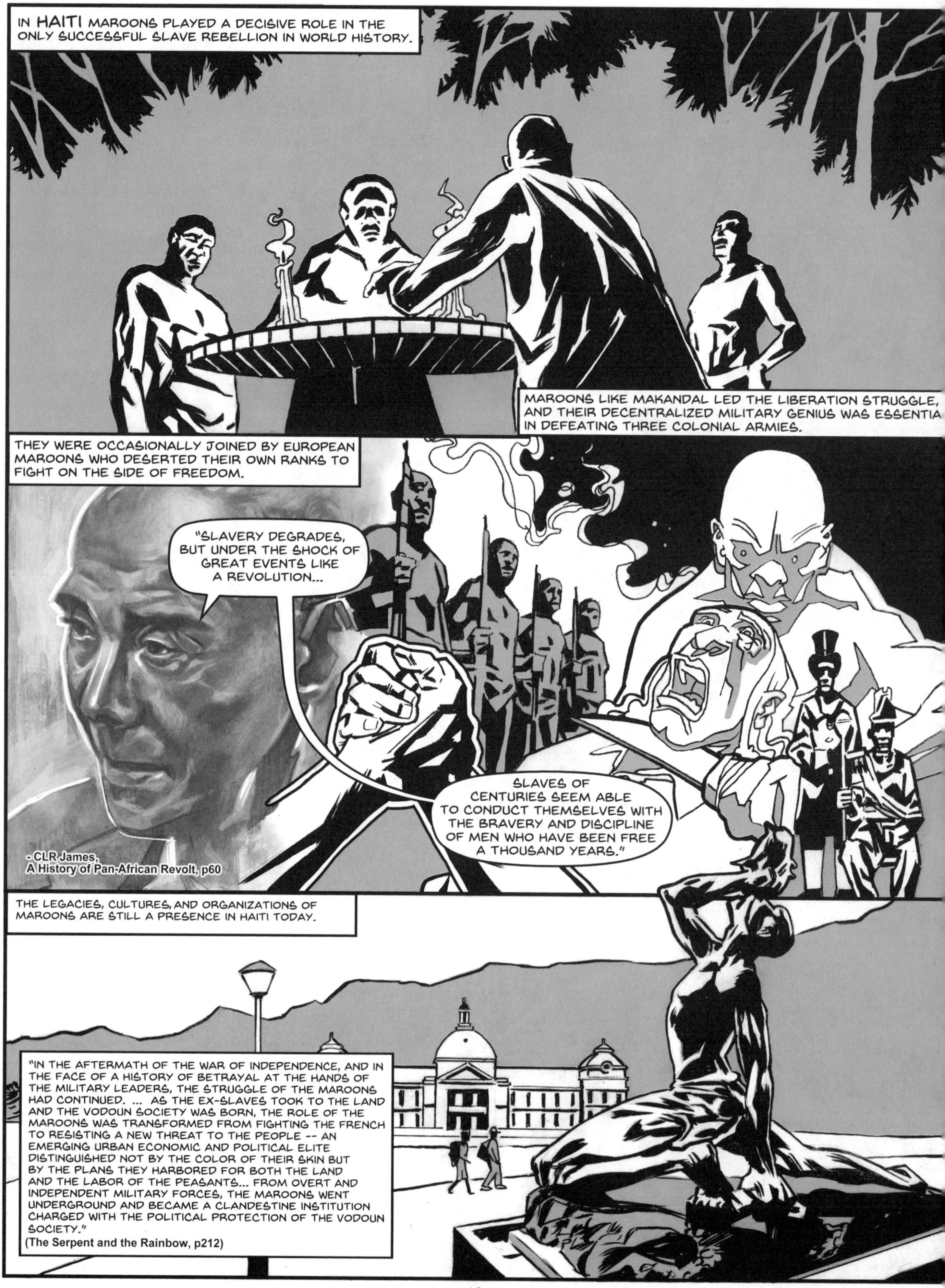
IN HAITI MAROONS PLAYED A DECISIVE ROLE IN THE ONLY SUCCESSFUL SLAVE REBELLION IN WORLD HISTORY.
MAROONS LIKE MAKANDAL LED THE LIBERATION STRUGGLE, AND THEIR DECENTRALIZED MILITARY GENIUS WAS ESSENTIA IN DEFEATING THREE COLONIAL ARMIES.
THEY WERE OCCASIONALLY JOINED BY EUROPEAN MAROONS WHO DESERTED THEIR OWN RANKS TO FIGHT ON THE SIDE OF FREEDOM.
"SLAVERY DEGRADES, BUT UNDER THE SHOCK OF GREAT EVENTS LIKE A REVOLUTION...
SLAVES OF CENTURIES SEEM ABLE TO CONDUCT THEMSELVES WITH THE BRAVERY AND DISCIPLINE OF MEN WHO HAVE BEEN FREE A THOUSAND YEARS."
- CLR James, A History of Pan-African Revolt, p60
THE LEGACIES, CULTURES, AND ORGANIZATIONS OF MAROONS ARE STILL A PRESENCE IN HAITI TODAY.
"IN THE AFTERMATH OF THE WAR OF INDEPENDENCE, AND IN THE FACE OF A HISTORY OF BETRAYAL AT THE HANDS OF THE MILITARY LEADERS, THE STRUGGLE OF THE MAROONS HAD CONTINUED. ... AS THE EX-SLAVES TOOK TO THE LAND AND THE VODOUN SOCIETY WAS BORN, THE ROLE OF THE MAROONS WAS TRANSFORMED FROM FIGHTING THE FRENCH TO RESISTING A NEW THREAT TO THE PEOPLE -- AN EMERGING URBAN ECONOMIC AND POLITICAL ELITE DISTINGUISHED NOT BY THE COLOR OF THEIR SKIN BUT BY THE PLANS THEY HARBORED FOR BOTH THE LAND AND THE LABOR OF THE PEASANTS... FROM OVERT AND INDEPENDENT MILITARY FORCES, THE MAROONS WENT UNDERGROUND AND BECAME A CLANDESTINE INSTITUTION CHARGED WITH THE POLITICAL PROTECTION OF THE VODOUN SOCIETY."
(The Serpent and the Rainbow, p212)

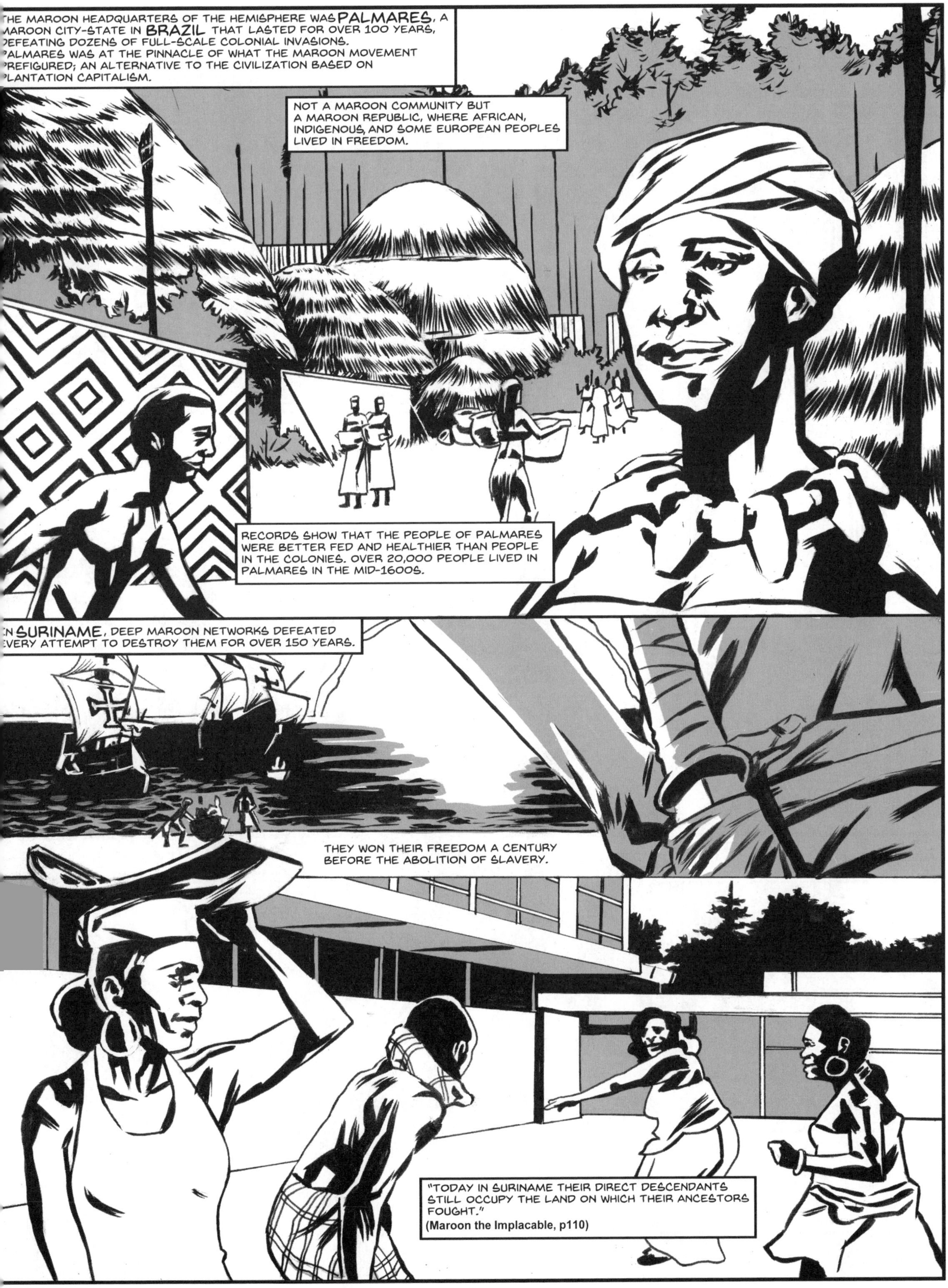
THE MAROON HEADQUARTERS OF THE HEMISPHERE WAS PALMARES, A MAROON CITY-STATE IN BRAZIL THAT LASTED FOR OVER 100 YEARS, DEFEATING DOZENS OF FULL-SCALE COLONIAL INVASIONS.
PALMARES WAS AT THE PINNACLE OF WHAT THE MAROON MOVEMENT PREFIGURED; AN ALTERNATIVE TO THE CIVILIZATION BASED ON PLANTATION CAPITALISM.
NOT A MAROON COMMUNITY BUT A MAROON REPUBLIC, WHERE AFRICAN, INDIGENOUS, AND SOME EUROPEAN PEOPLES LIVED IN FREEDOM.
RECORDS SHOW THAT THE PEOPLE OF PALMARES WERE BETTER FED AND HEALTHIER THAN PEOPLE IN THE COLONIES. OVER 20,000 PEOPLE LIVED IN PALMARES IN THE MID-1600S.
IN SURINAME, DEEP MAROON NETWORKS DEFEATED EVERY ATTEMPT TO DESTROY THEM FOR OVER 150 YEARS.
THEY WON THEIR FREEDOM A CENTURY BEFORE THE ABOLITION OF SLAVERY.
"TODAY IN SURINAME THEIR DIRECT DESCENDANTS STILL OCCUPY THE LAND ON WHICH THEIR ANCESTORS FOUGHT."
(Maroon the Implacable, p110)

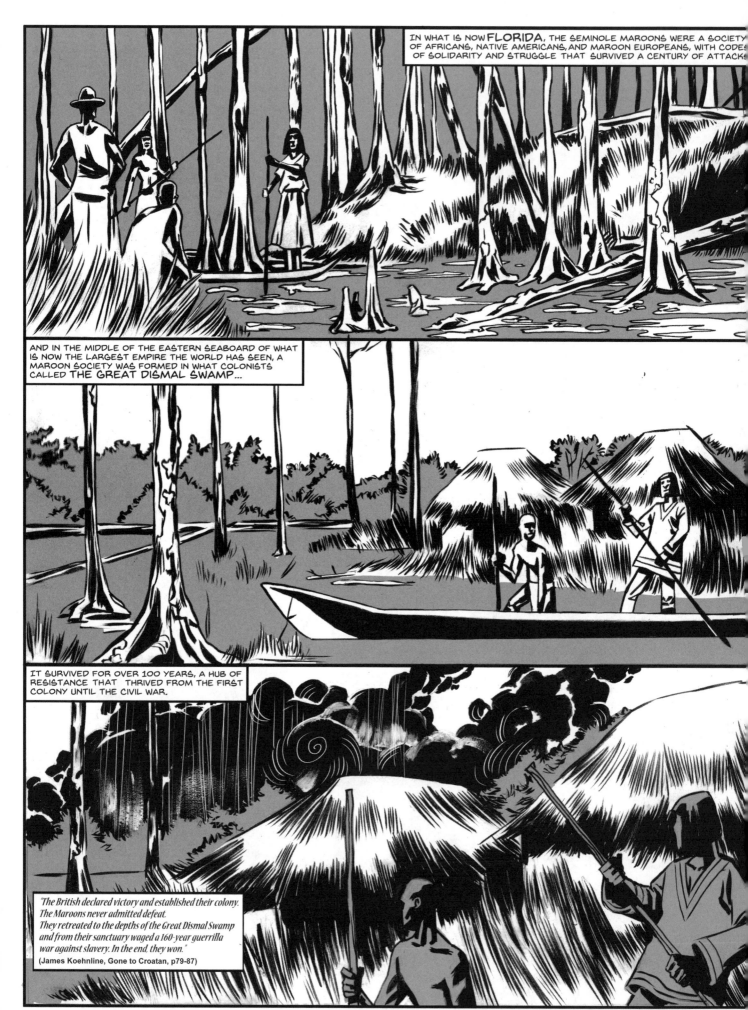

IN WHAT IS NOW **FLORIDA**, THE SEMINOLE MAROONS WERE A SOCIETY OF AFRICANS, NATIVE AMERICANS, AND MAROON EUROPEANS, WITH CODES OF SOLIDARITY AND STRUGGLE THAT SURVIVED A CENTURY OF ATTACKS.

AND IN THE MIDDLE OF THE EASTERN SEABOARD OF WHAT IS NOW THE LARGEST EMPIRE THE WORLD HAS SEEN, A MAROON SOCIETY WAS FORMED IN WHAT COLONISTS CALLED **THE GREAT DISMAL SWAMP**...

IT SURVIVED FOR OVER 100 YEARS, A HUB OF RESISTANCE THAT THRIVED FROM THE FIRST COLONY UNTIL THE CIVIL WAR.

"The British declared victory and established their colony.
The Maroons never admitted defeat.
They retreated to the depths of the Great Dismal Swamp and from their sanctuary waged a 160-year guerrilla war against slavery. In the end, they won."
(James Koehnline, Gone to Croatan, p79-87)

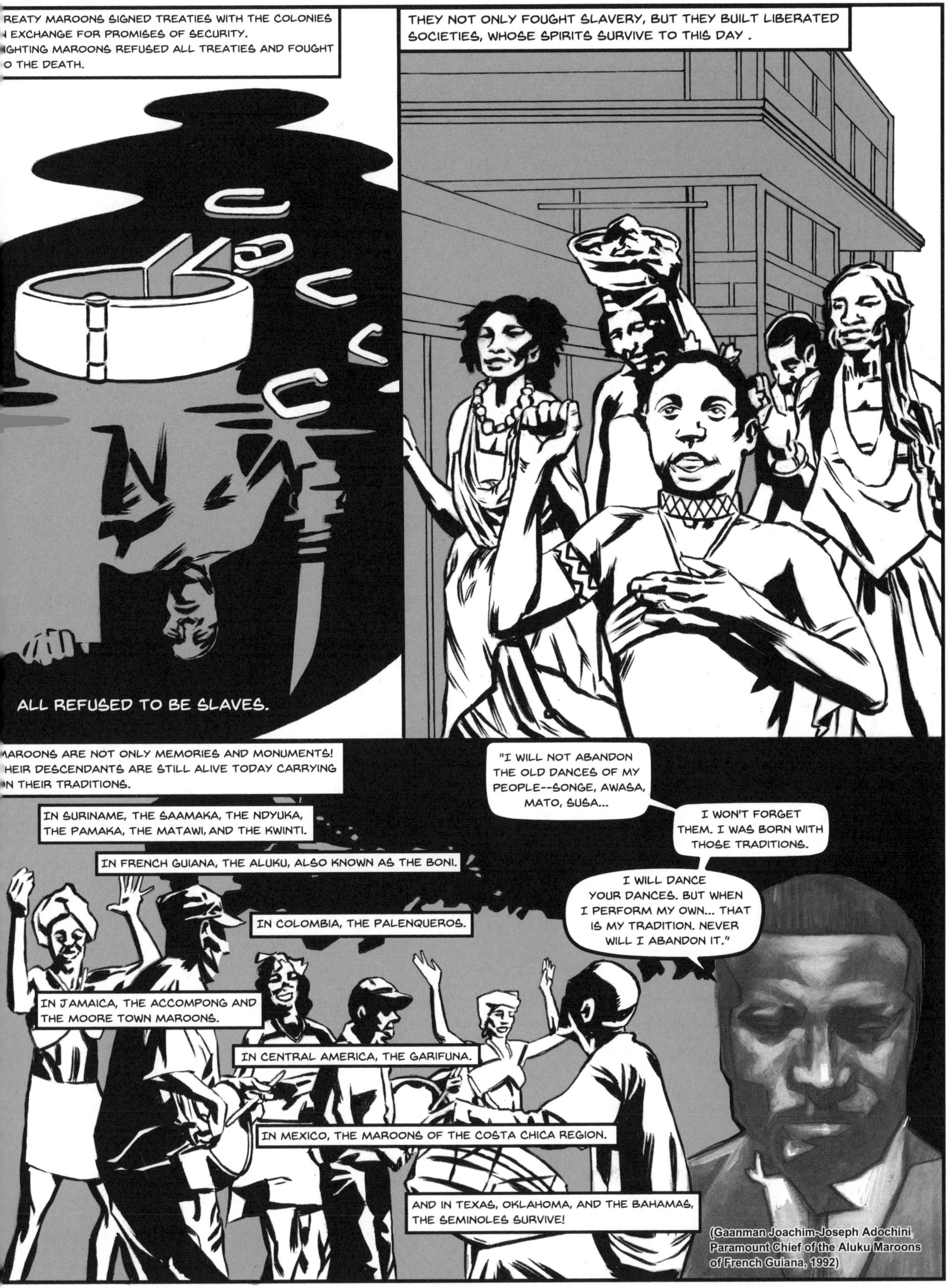

REATY MAROONS SIGNED TREATIES WITH THE COLONIES
N EXCHANGE FOR PROMISES OF SECURITY.
IGHTING MAROONS REFUSED ALL TREATIES AND FOUGHT
O THE DEATH.
ALL REFUSED TO BE SLAVES.
THEY NOT ONLY FOUGHT SLAVERY, BUT THEY BUILT LIBERATED SOCIETIES, WHOSE SPIRITS SURVIVE TO THIS DAY .
AAROONS ARE NOT ONLY MEMORIES AND MONUMENTS!
HEIR DESCENDANTS ARE STILL ALIVE TODAY CARRYING
N THEIR TRADITIONS.
IN SURINAME, THE SAAMAKA, THE NDYUKA, THE PAMAKA, THE MATAWI, AND THE KWINTI.
IN FRENCH GUIANA, THE ALUKU, ALSO KNOWN AS THE BONI.
IN COLOMBIA, THE PALENQUEROS.
IN JAMAICA, THE ACCOMPONG AND THE MOORE TOWN MAROONS.
IN CENTRAL AMERICA, THE GARIFUNA.
IN MEXICO, THE MAROONS OF THE COSTA CHICA REGION.
AND IN TEXAS, OKLAHOMA, AND THE BAHAMAS, THE SEMINOLES SURVIVE!
"I WILL NOT ABANDON THE OLD DANCES OF MY PEOPLE--SONGE, AWASA, MATO, SUSA...
I WON'T FORGET THEM. I WAS BORN WITH THOSE TRADITIONS.
I WILL DANCE YOUR DANCES. BUT WHEN I PERFORM MY OWN... THAT IS MY TRADITION. NEVER WILL I ABANDON IT."
(Gaanman Joachim-Joseph Adochini, Paramount Chief of the Aluku Maroons of French Guiana, 1992)

I Am Maroon!

illustrated by Mac McGill

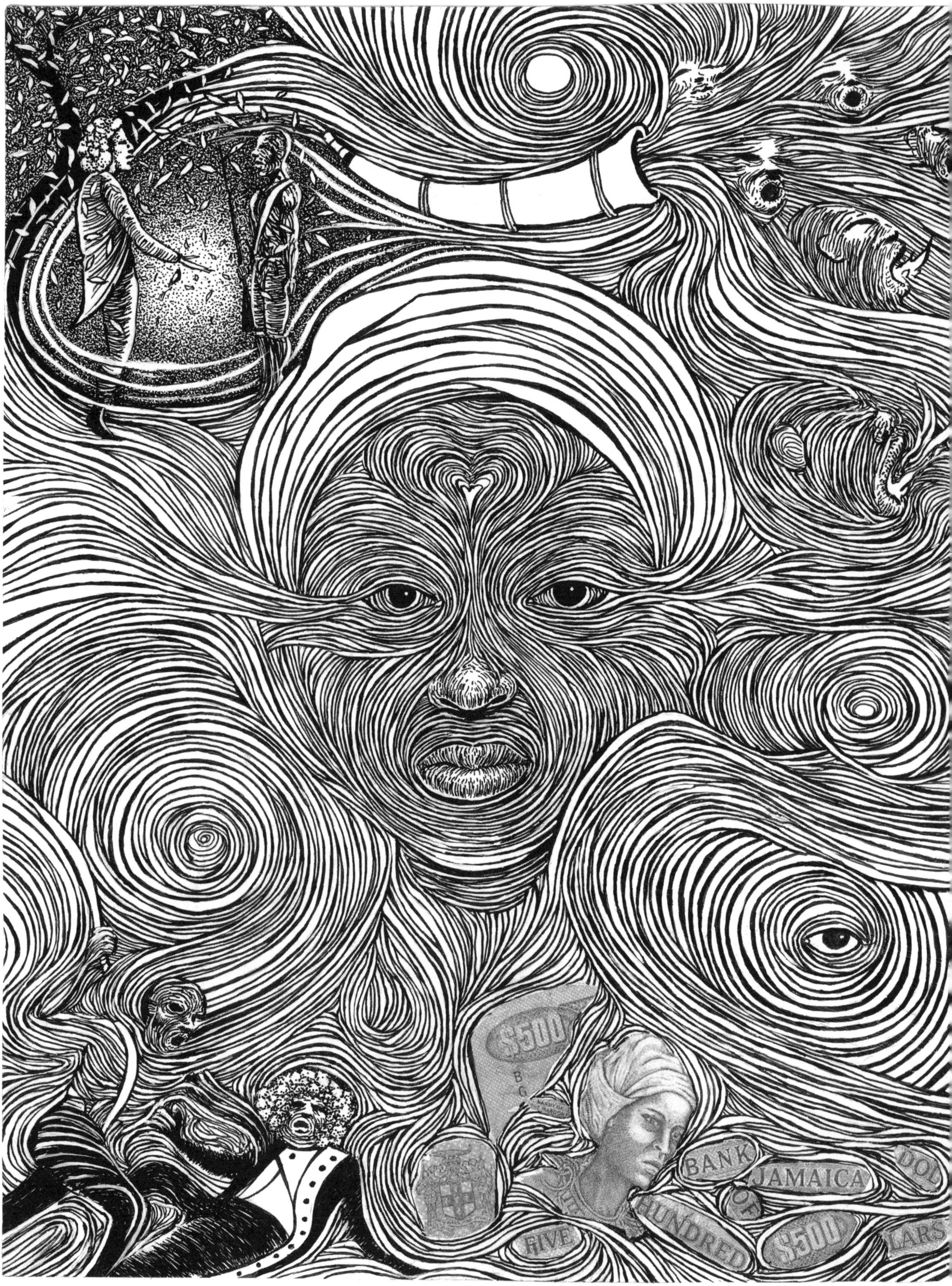
$500
BANK
OF
JAMAICA
DOL
LARS
FIVE
HUNDRED
$500

GRANNY NANNY

"The legendary 'Granny Nanny' of eighteenth-century Jamaica is variously recognized as a female guerrilla leader, guerrilla spiritual leader (Obia or Obeah), a freedom fighter who has a town named in her honor in the maroons' 'liberated territory.' There may have been more than one Nanny. . . . At this time in Jamaica, Nanny is looked upon as a national hero. . . . Nanny Town became the center of the resistance to British plantation imperialism in Jamaica, the headquarters from which the maroon bands almost succeeded in driving all of the imperialists from the island altogether." [*Maroon the Implacable*, p32 and 114]

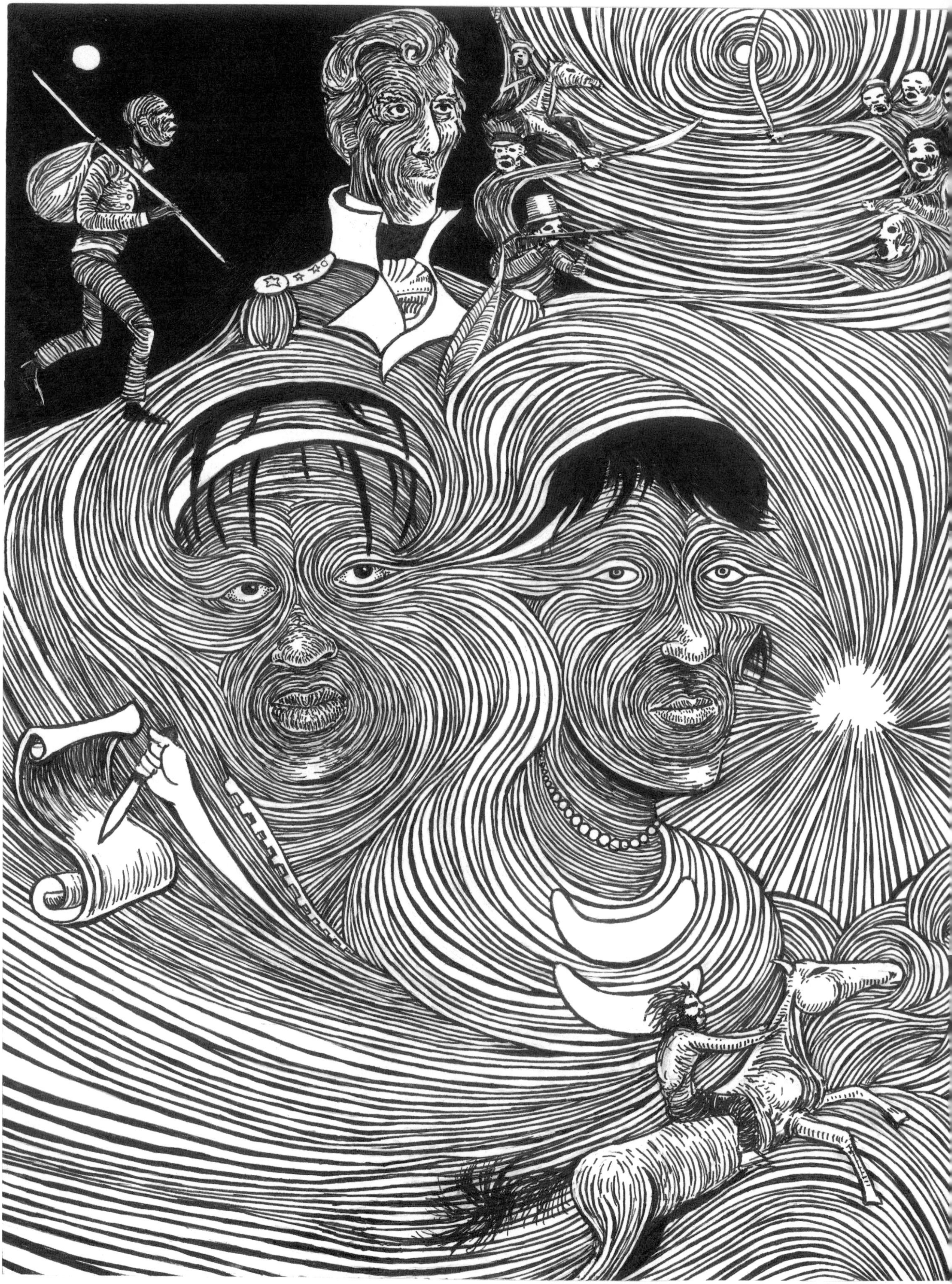

OSCEOLA AND JOHN HORSE

In present-day Florida, for over a hundred years, African, indigenous, and some European maroons joined together in resistance to slavery and colonization and became known as the Seminoles.

Born in 1804 into Creek, Scots-Irish, and English lineage, Osceola was a Seminole maroon who fought against the armies of Andrew Jackson in what are known as the "Indian Wars." These were really slave-catching expeditions, designed to eliminate the maroons. The bond formed between European, indigenous, and Africans was legendary: "any Amerindian Seminoles who tried to deliver Africans into slavery were to be killed by their own people. History's most recognized Amerindian Seminole, Osceola, showed where he stood by killing a powerful Amerindian Seminole chief when it was discovered that the latter had broken the pact." (*Maroon the Implacable*, p147)

John Horse, a Seminole of African descent, was born around 1812 and became a military adviser to Osceola. When Osceola was captured and their people were surrounded but undefeated, John Horse led an Exodus, a Long March of prophetic proportions, from Florida to Oklahoma to Mexico, with the Seminoles defending themselves the whole way. Having achieved freedom at last in Mexico, John Horse became a captain in the Mexican army. "Today the Seminoles' descendants can be found in Oklahoma, Texas, and Mexico—all still fiercely proud of their distinct history and heritage, with many still speaking their own pidgin dialects and practicing their own customs." (*Maroon the Implacable*, p150)

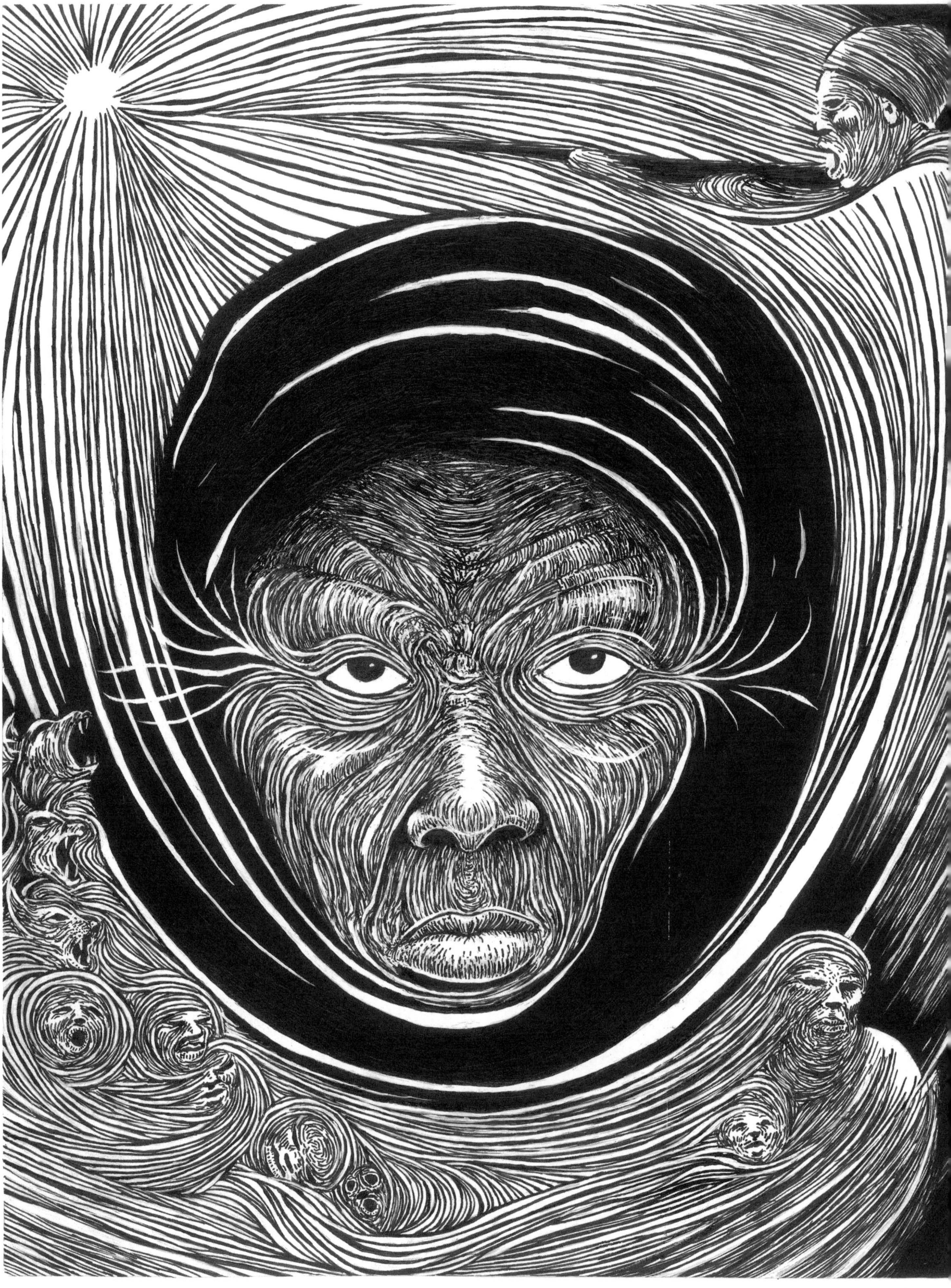

HARRIET TUBMAN

Born into slavery, Harriet Tubman escaped in her twenties and went on to lead a struggle that liberated a continent. Five feet tall, illiterate, and suffering from hypersomnia—the result of a fractured skull due to abuse as a slave—her record as warrior, healer, and political leader are unsurpassed. An expert in disguise and daring, she organized and led nineteen separate raids into the South to lead the enslaved to freedom. When the Civil War began, she was the first woman on the battlefields and in the hospitals, leading the Union army to numerous victories and caring for the sick and wounded in the aftermath. Abolitionist leaders called her "the General." She never retired. After the end of the war, she dedicated herself to building a liberated and communal homestead in Auburn, New York. She never had an official title or received a salary; "having no power, she could live with unmeasureable power." (*Jailbreak Out of History: The Re-Biography of Harriet Tubman*)

"I freed a thousand slaves. I could have freed a thousand more if they only they knew they were slaves. . . . I never ran my train off the track, and I never lost a passenger." (The Harriet Tubman Home in Auburn New York)

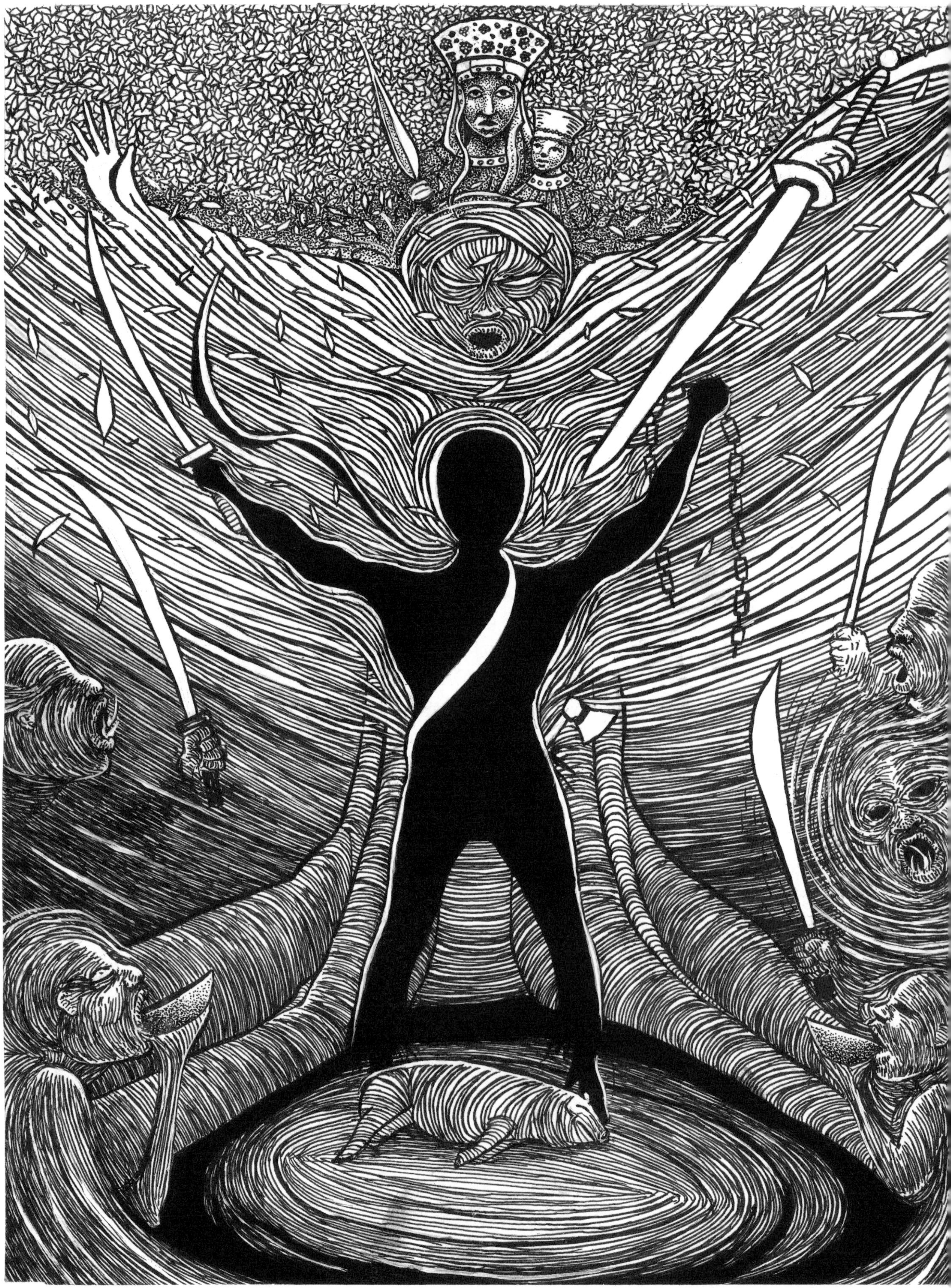

Ezili Dantor, Cécile Fatiman, and Dutty Boukman

In 1791, in Bois Caïman, Haiti, the warrior love goddess and "Mother of Haiti" Ezili Dantor possessed the Haitian high priestess, mambo Cécile Fatiman. She then crowned the African revolutionary maroon and houngan Dutty Boukman with her scepter, invoking and convoking the Haitian revolution.

"One dark night, a large assembly of the colony's Africans met at a secret ceremony on a mountain, including both enslaved workers and maroon guerrillas. They represented thousands of other Africans—both on the many plantations and in the fugitive communities in the mountains. The ceremony and last-minute plans were being overseen by Boukman and an enslaved female—both Vodun (Voodoo) spiritual leaders . . . when the revolt was launched shortly thereafter, it was led by scores of decentralized bands of African workers and maroon guerrilla groups. . . .

"Before the well-known Toussaint L'Ouverture appeared on the stage, the Haitian revolution was being led by figures that the decentralized groups propelled forward: the maroons Jean-François, Biassou, and Lamour Derance; and the rebel-enslaved workers Romaine the Prophetess and Hyacinthe, the fearless leader of the battle of Croix des Bouquets. The mulattos had a number of their own independent groups and distinguished leaders. In addition, there was also a small segment of whites who were in league with the anti-slavery wing of the French Jacobins, and who loosely allied themselves with one rebel group or another.

"Within two years of the beginning of the French Revolution, and continuing for twelve harrowing years, the Haitian revolutionaries would go on to militarily engage and defeat first their colonial enslavers, then a succession of armies fielded by Spain and England—as well as a traitorous mulatto army and finally tens of thousands of Napoleon Bonaparte's veteran French 'revolutionary' troops. The victorious Africans would go on to found the country of Haiti in 1803–1804, the only country in world history established by formerly enslaved workers."
(*Maroon the Implacable*, p118–119)

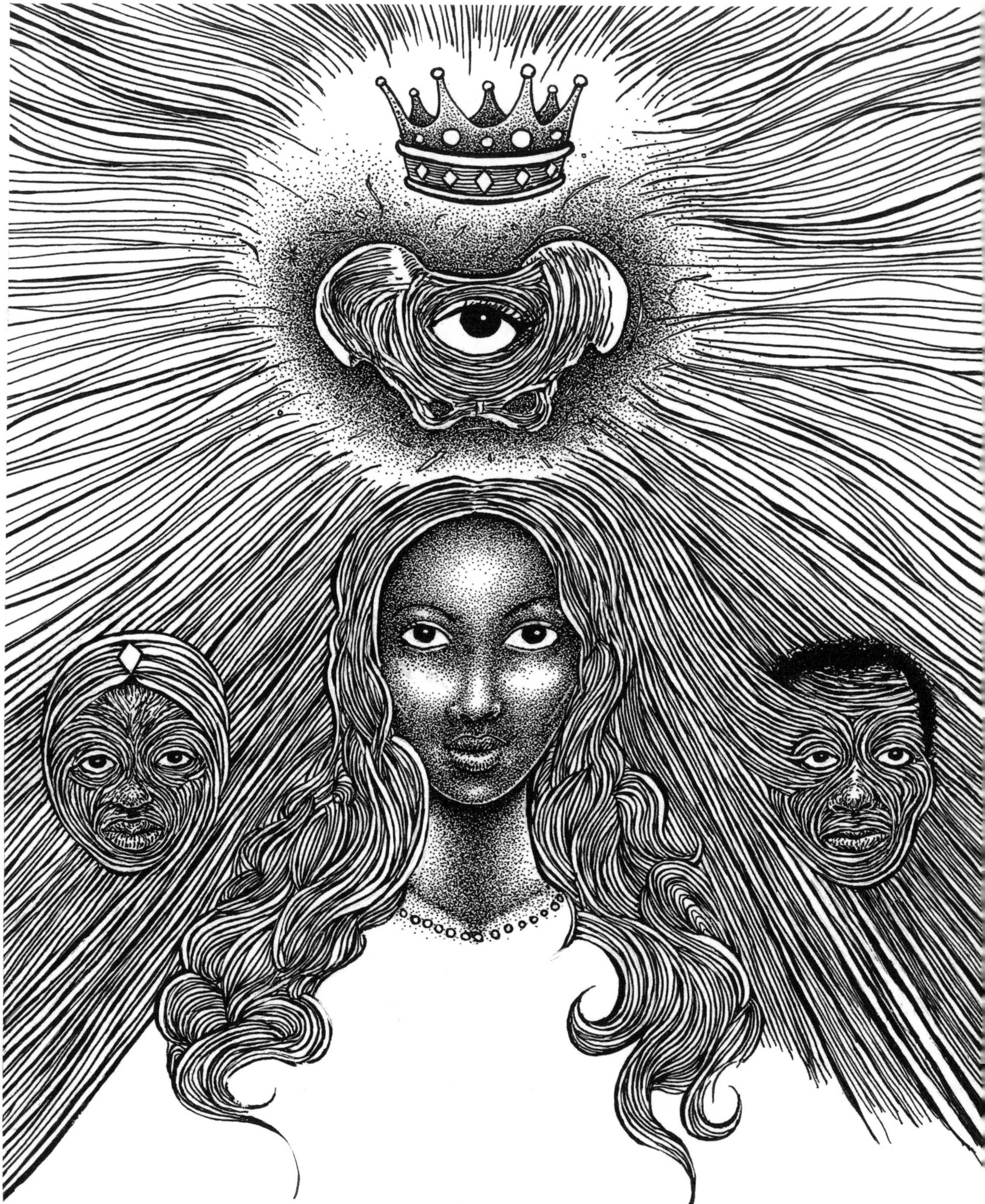

María Lionza, King Miguel, and
José Leonardo Chirino

María Lionza is revered in Venezuela, and her spirit is said to inhabit the mountains outside Yaracuy. Born to an indigenous chief, she has become immortalized in a pantheon of maroon spirits: also in her holy trinity are the indigenous chief Guaicaipuro and the African warrior Negro Felipe, both of whom lived and died fighting against the Spanish colonists. A goddess of nature, she represents a synthesis of African, indigenous, and European maroon cultures.

In 1552, an enslaved African named Miguel brought from Puerto Rico to Venezuela to work in the mines escaped into the mountains. After assembling a maroon society with the indigenous Jirajara and Gayones peoples, he led an uprising against slavery, becoming known as King Miguel, alongside his wife Queen Giomar. Though he died in battle, his struggle marked the first uprising of the Afro-Venezuelan people.

José Leonardo Chirino was born in 1754 to an indigenous mother and an enslaved black father. Growing up free, he traveled to Haiti and witnessed the revolution. In 1795, he led a mass insurrection of indigenous and African maroons, with demands linked to those of the Haitian and French Revolutions.

Today in Venezuela, the history and heritage of maroons are celebrated and continued as part of an ongoing revolutionary process.

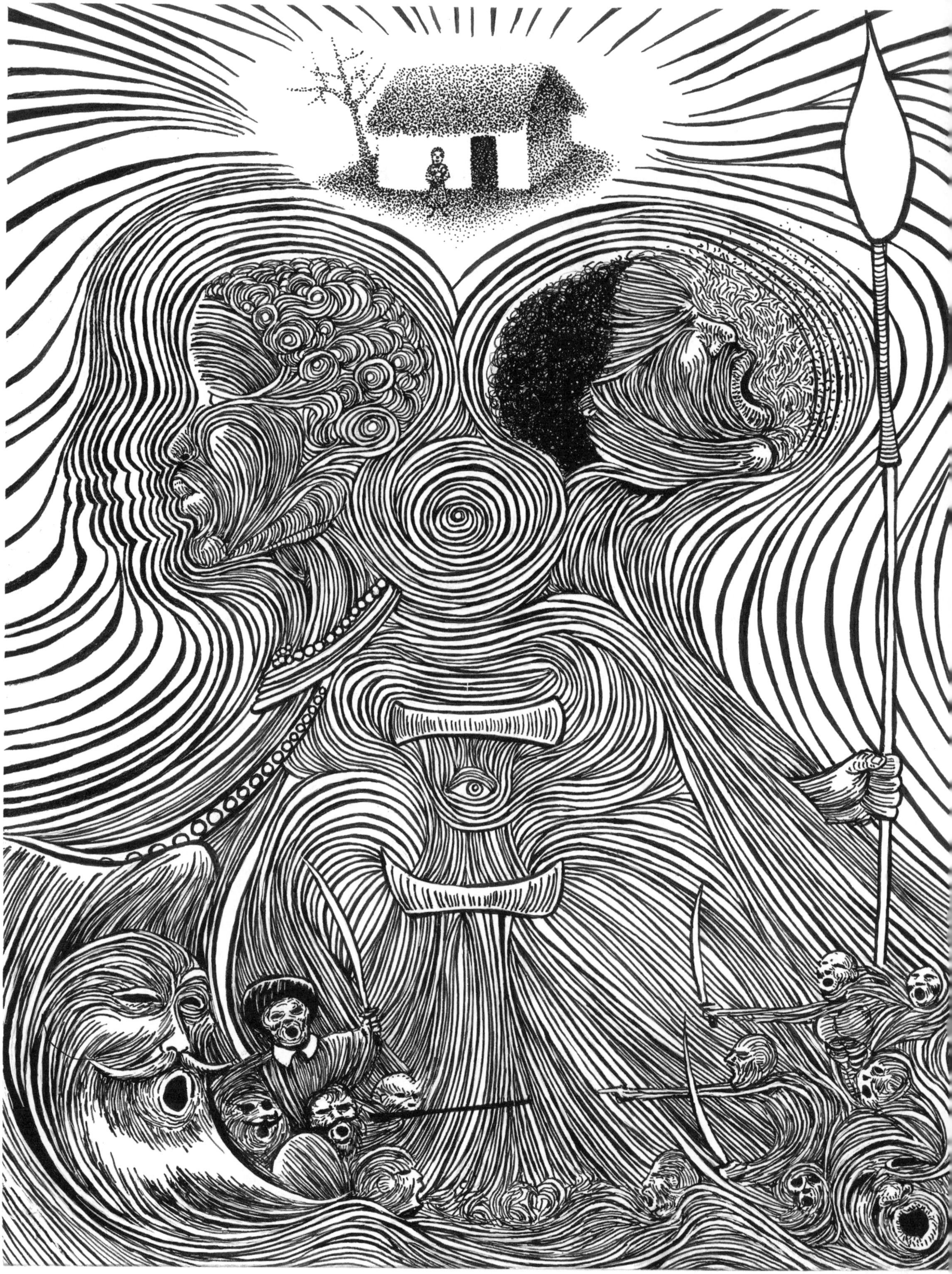

GANGA ZUMBA AND ZUMBI

Ganga Zumba was king of Palmares, the maroon capital of the Western Hemisphere. Ganga Zumba united a dozen maroon communities into the great Quilombo dos Palmares, with tens of thousands of citizens. In the 1670s, Ganga Zumba's compound contained 1,500 houses.

Zumbi, born free in Palmares, was kidnapped at six years old and held captive by the church. At the age of fifteen, he escaped and returned to Palmares. In 1678, when Ganga Zumba signed a treaty with the Portuguese in search of peace, Zumbi led a revolt against him.

Their split illustrates the recurring political divide in maroon societies between "treaty maroons" and "fighting maroons." Zumbi was the last leader of Palmares before its final destruction by the Portuguese. While the Quilombo dos Palmares was gone, maroon resistance in the region carried on for another century.

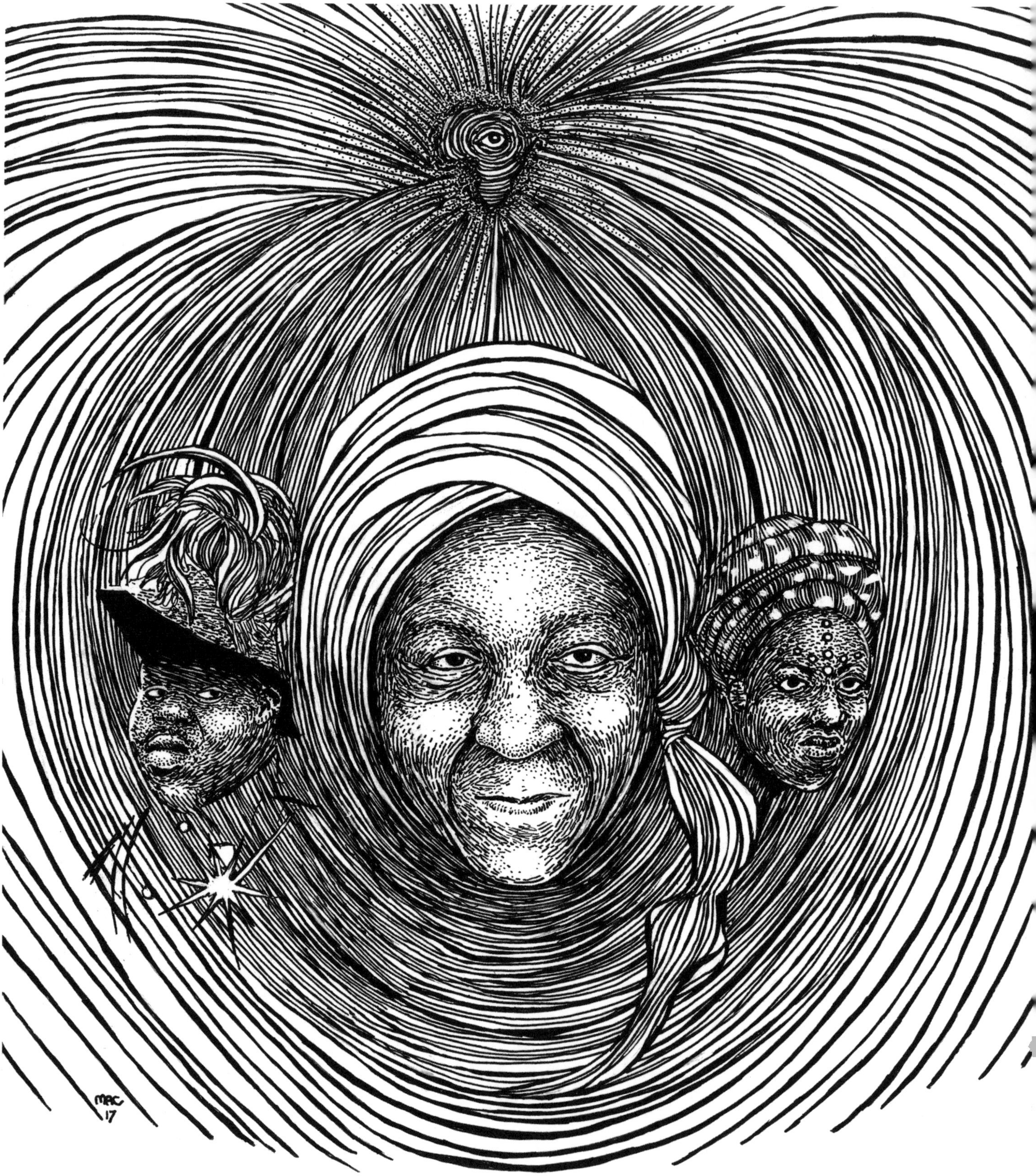
MAC
17

QUEEN MOTHER MOORE

Queen Mother (Audley) Moore transcended traditional amerikan or Afrikan politics, bridging continents, historical periods, and peoples. Born in 1898 in New Iberia, Louisiana, her grandmother had been enslaved at birth and her grandfather lynched. An early follower of Marcus Garvey, Moore went on to be a founder and leader of the Universal Association of Ethiopian Women, the Committee for Reparations for Descendants of U.S. Slaves, and the Republic of New Afrika, advocating for land and self-determination for all people of African heritage. During the first of many visits to Africa, she was given the honorific title of Queen Mother by the Ashanti people of Ghana. Decades later, she was an invited guest at the South African/ Azanian ceremonies celebrating the release of Madiba Nelson Mandela. A Bishop in the Apostolic Orthodox Church of Judea, Moore—based most of her life in Harlem and Brooklyn, New York—was a true internationalist and freedom fighter, fiercely independent and self-sufficient.

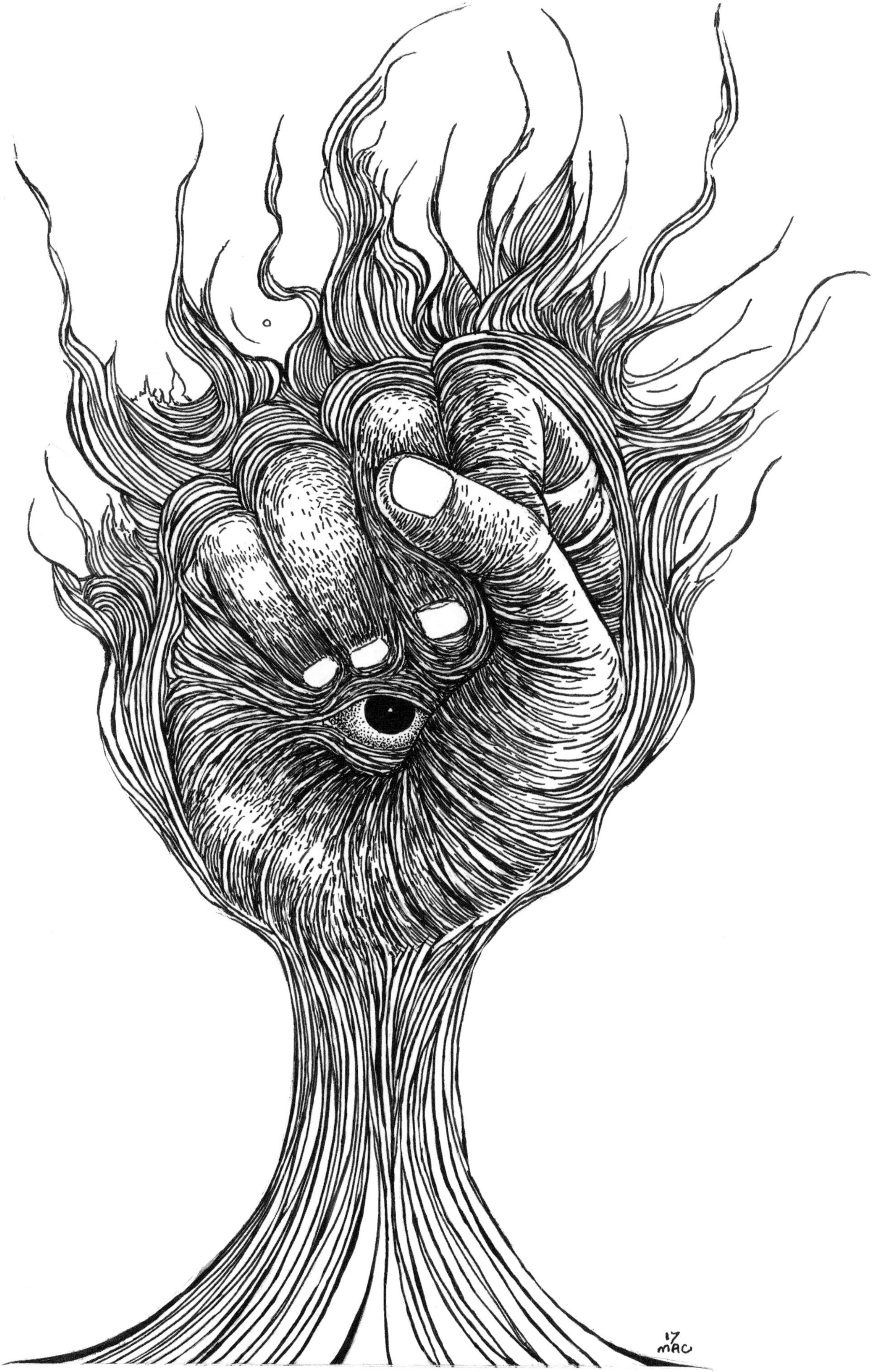
17
MAC

THE BLACK LIBERATION ARMY

The Black Liberation Army, alongside related forces of self-defense and self-determination, led clandestine armed struggles within the u.s. empire throughout the late 1960s and 1970s.

"The Black Liberation Army was not a centralized, organized group with a common leadership and chain of command. Instead there were various organizations and collectives working together and simultaneously independent of each other." —Assata Shakur

Explicitly anti-capitalist, anti-imperialist, anti-racist, and anti-sexist, the legacy of the Black Liberation Army and their allies continues to inspire and influence liberation movements around the world. Many Black Liberation Army combatants and supporters are still imprisoned after forty or more years. Today, modern maroons everywhere inherit their struggle for freedom. Free Sundiata Acoli, Mutulu Shakur, Leonard Peltier, Mumia Abu Jamal, the Move 9, Imam Jamil Al-Amin, Jalil Muntaqim, Veronza Bowers, Kamau Sadiki, David Gilbert, Robert Seth Hayes, Ruchell Cinque Magee, and FREE ALL POLITICAL PRISONERS!

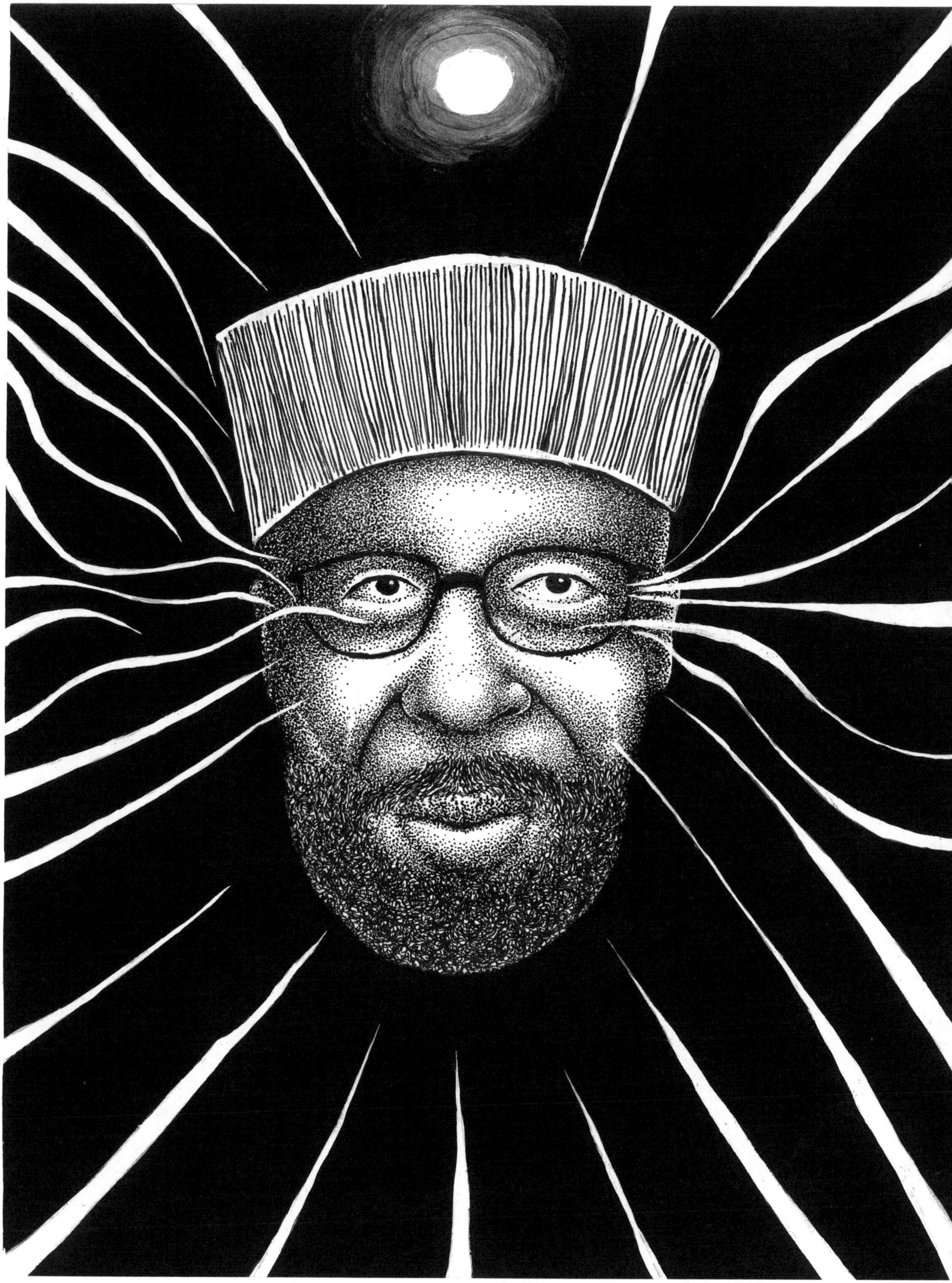

RUSSELL MAROON SHOATZ

"I'm writing these words from a prison. Don't get bent out of shape about that, because I'm actually freer than many of you. . . . Many have asked why I call myself "Maroon." . . . In 1977, I escaped from the State Prison in Huntington, Pennsylvania. I lived off the land for twenty-seven days while trying to evade scores of state police, prison personnel, FBI agents, and local police and volunteers. I had cause to reflect on and gain courage from all the freedom fighters I'd read about and this did much to guide and reinforce my determination to succeed. However, I was recaptured and on my return to prison, a friend mentioned that he had kept up with the search through the press. After a while he said, "They were chasing you like a maroon!" . . . As I gradually began to learn about the maroons, I became inspired by these audacious fighters and the nickname "Maroon" became a badge of pride and a constant source of spiritual inspiration. . . . Rest easy, fighting maroons. There are many now and to come who will derive inspiration from your valorous examples—inspiration that will "arm their spirits" to fight the good fight . . . till victory or death!!! . . . I am Maroon!" (*Maroon the Implacable*, p40 and 31–35)

The Dragon or the Hydra?

written and illustrated by Seth Tobocman

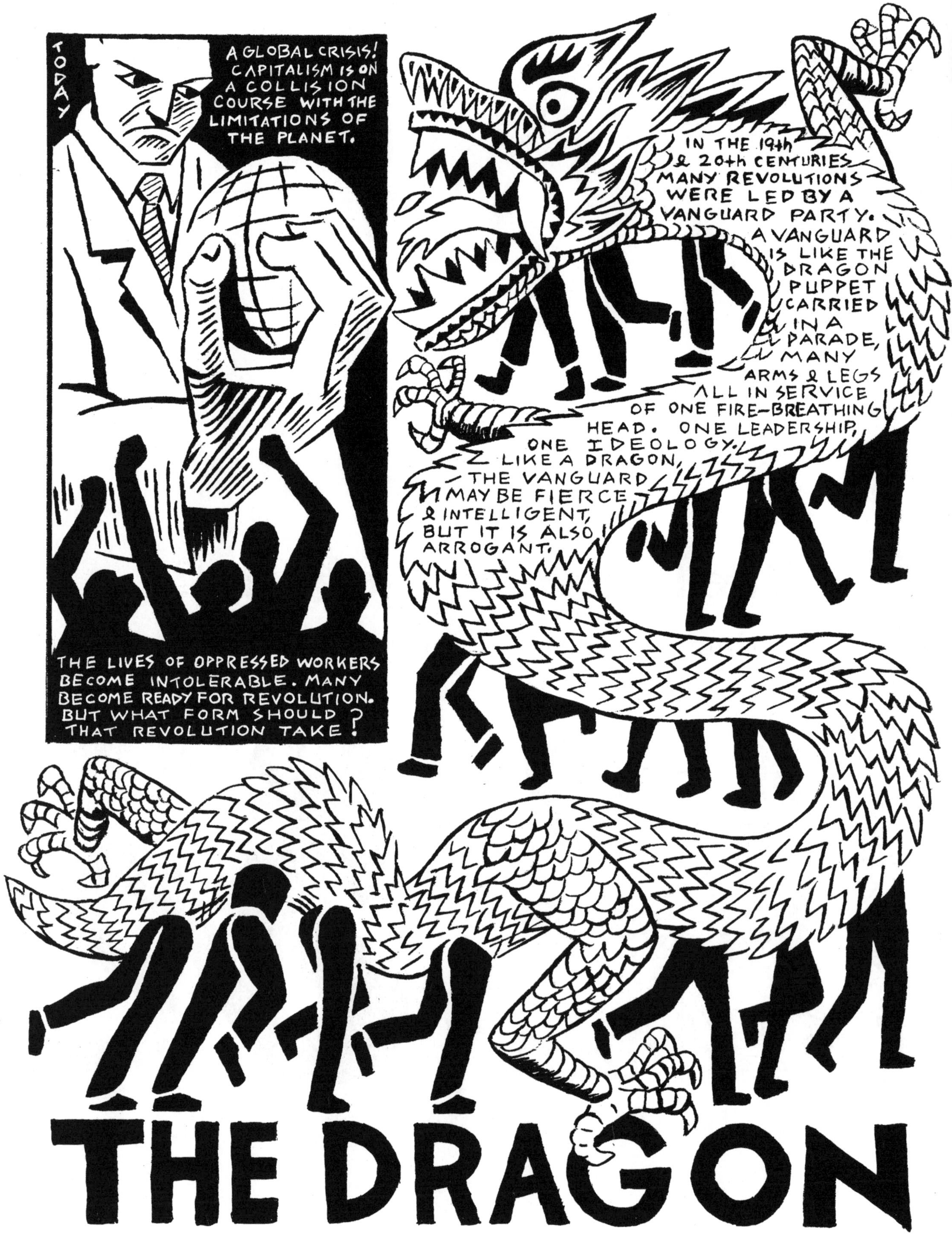
TODAY
A GLOBAL CRISIS! CAPITALISM IS ON A COLLISION COURSE WITH THE LIMITATIONS OF THE PLANET.
THE LIVES OF OPPRESSED WORKERS BECOME INTOLERABLE. MANY BECOME READY FOR REVOLUTION. BUT WHAT FORM SHOULD THAT REVOLUTION TAKE?
IN THE 19th & 20th CENTURIES MANY REVOLUTIONS WERE LED BY A VANGUARD PARTY. A VANGUARD IS LIKE THE DRAGON PUPPET CARRIED IN A PARADE, MANY ARMS & LEGS ALL IN SERVICE OF ONE FIRE-BREATHING HEAD. ONE LEADERSHIP, ONE IDEOLOGY. LIKE A DRAGON, THE VANGUARD MAY BE FIERCE & INTELLIGENT, BUT IT IS ALSO ARROGANT.
THE DRAGON

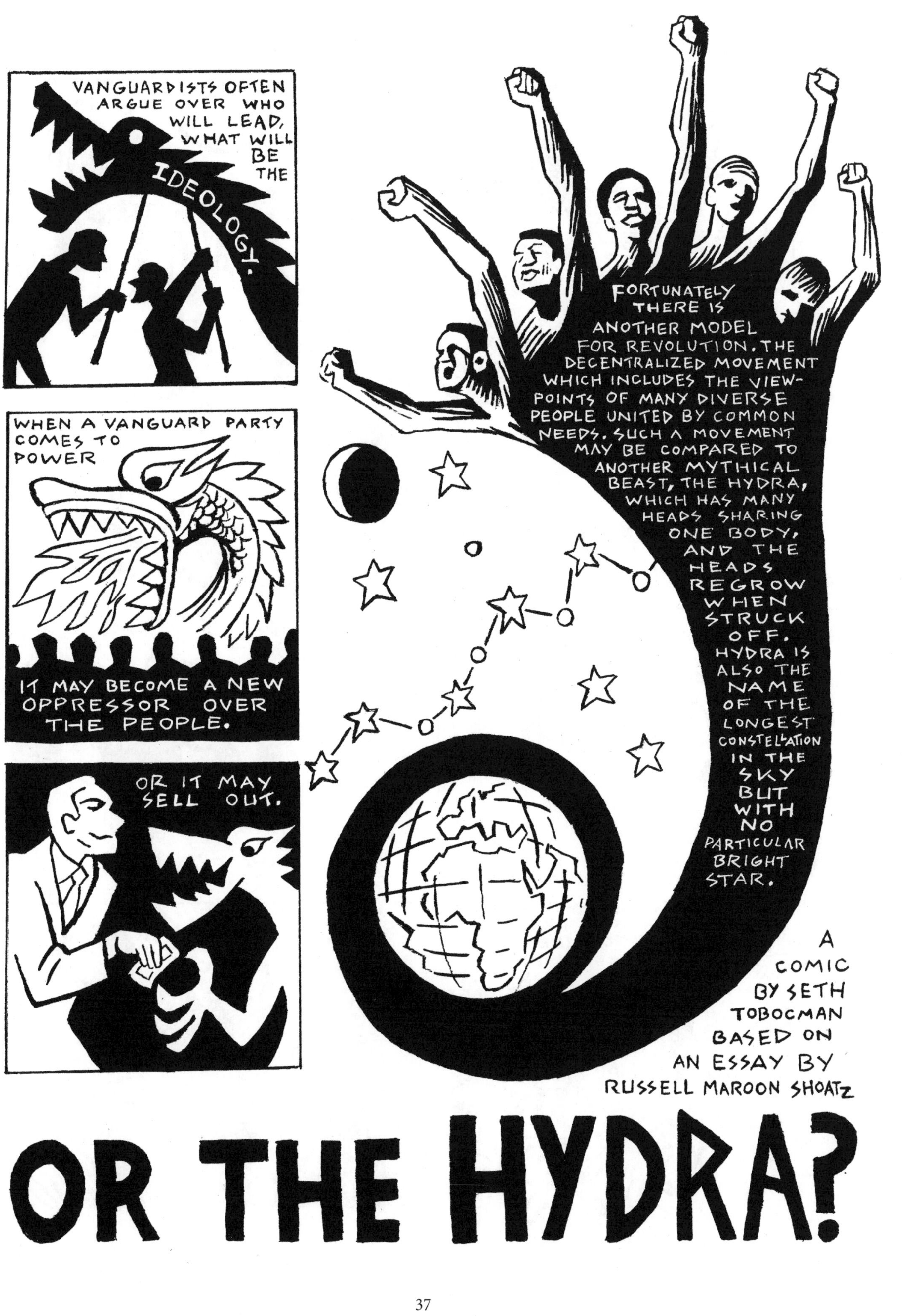
VANGUARDISTS OFTEN ARGUE OVER WHO WILL LEAD, WHAT WILL BE THE
IDEOLOGY.
WHEN A VANGUARD PARTY COMES TO POWER
IT MAY BECOME A NEW OPPRESSOR OVER THE PEOPLE.
OR IT MAY SELL OUT.
FORTUNATELY THERE IS ANOTHER MODEL FOR REVOLUTION. THE DECENTRALIZED MOVEMENT WHICH INCLUDES THE VIEWPOINTS OF MANY DIVERSE PEOPLE UNITED BY COMMON NEEDS. SUCH A MOVEMENT MAY BE COMPARED TO ANOTHER MYTHICAL BEAST, THE HYDRA, WHICH HAS MANY HEADS SHARING ONE BODY, AND THE HEADS REGROW WHEN STRUCK OFF. HYDRA IS ALSO THE NAME OF THE LONGEST CONSTELLATION IN THE SKY BUT WITH NO PARTICULAR BRIGHT STAR.
A COMIC BY SETH TOBOCMAN BASED ON AN ESSAY BY RUSSELL MAROON SHOATZ

OR THE HYDRA?

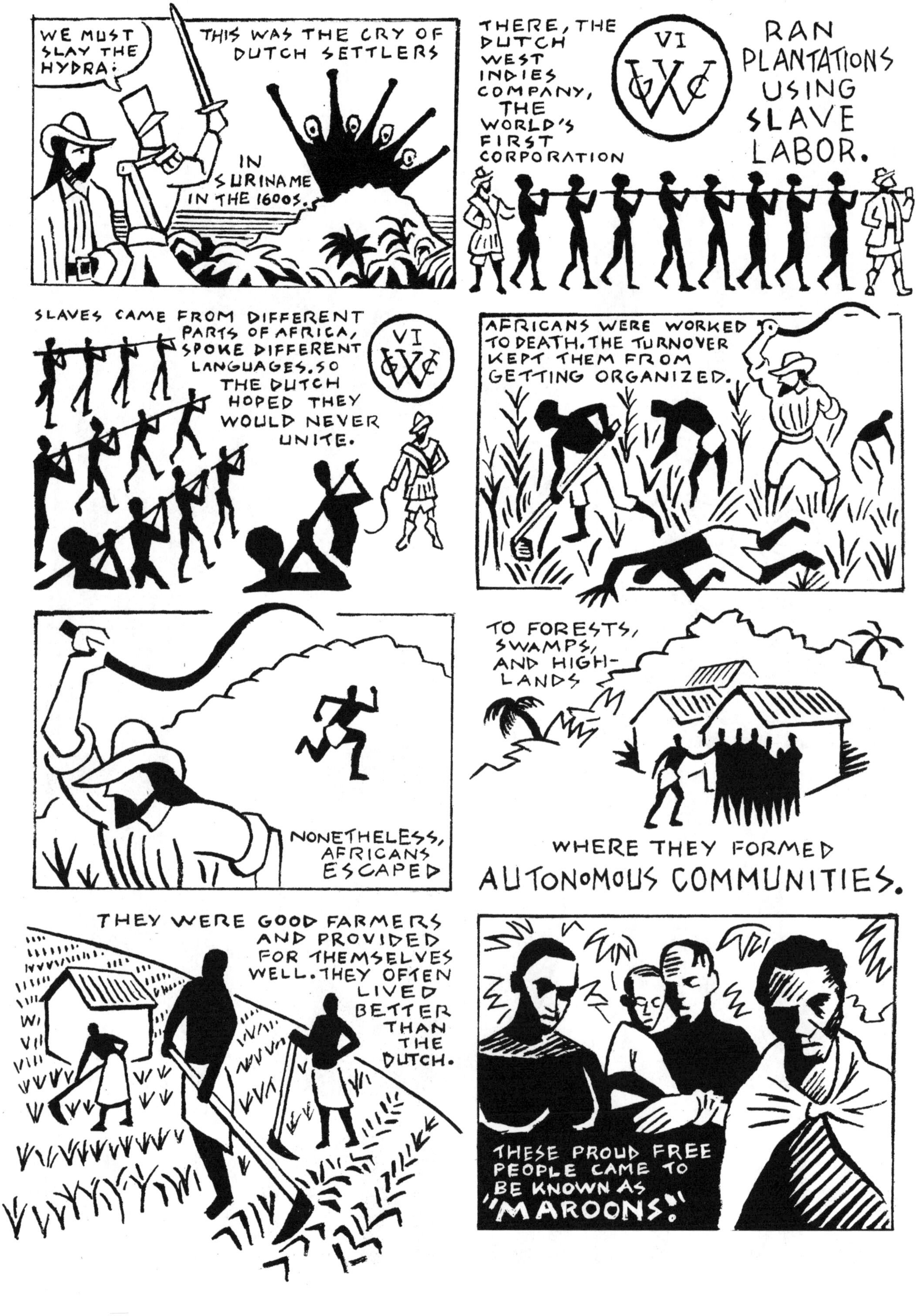
WE MUST SLAY THE HYDRA!
THIS WAS THE CRY OF DUTCH SETTLERS
IN SURINAME IN THE 1600S.
THERE, THE DUTCH WEST INDIES COMPANY, THE WORLD'S FIRST CORPORATION
VI WC
RAN PLANTATIONS USING SLAVE LABOR.
SLAVES CAME FROM DIFFERENT PARTS OF AFRICA, SPOKE DIFFERENT LANGUAGES. SO THE DUTCH HOPED THEY WOULD NEVER UNITE.
VI WC
AFRICANS WERE WORKED TO DEATH. THE TURNOVER KEPT THEM FROM GETTING ORGANIZED.
NONETHELESS, AFRICANS ESCAPED
TO FORESTS, SWAMPS, AND HIGH-LANDS
WHERE THEY FORMED AUTONOMOUS COMMUNITIES.
THEY WERE GOOD FARMERS AND PROVIDED FOR THEMSELVES WELL. THEY OFTEN LIVED BETTER THAN THE DUTCH.
THESE PROUD FREE PEOPLE CAME TO BE KNOWN AS "MAROONS."

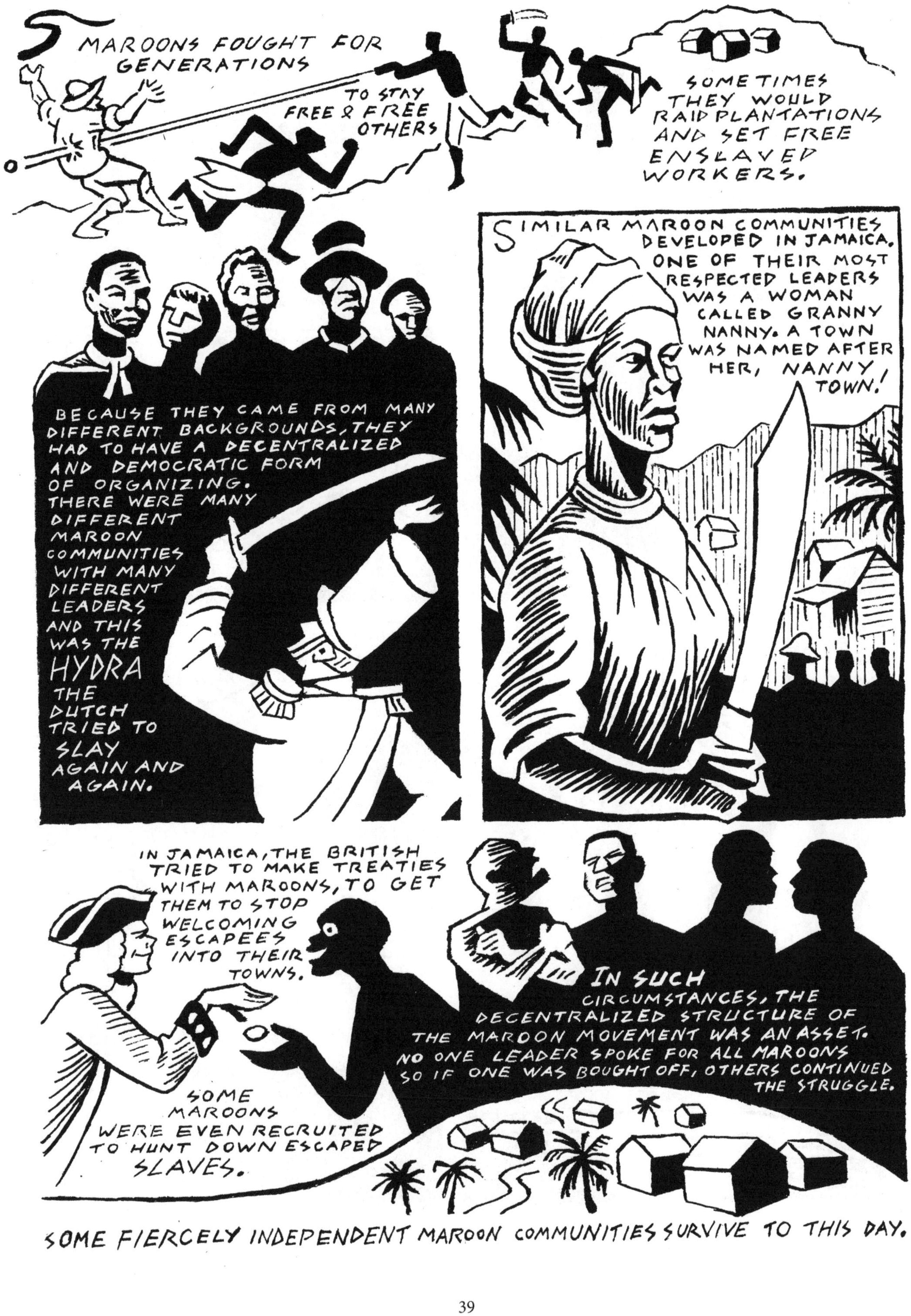

MAROONS FOUGHT FOR GENERATIONS
TO STAY FREE & FREE OTHERS
SOMETIMES THEY WOULD RAID PLANTATIONS AND SET FREE ENSLAVED WORKERS.
BECAUSE THEY CAME FROM MANY DIFFERENT BACKGROUNDS, THEY HAD TO HAVE A DECENTRALIZED AND DEMOCRATIC FORM OF ORGANIZING. THERE WERE MANY DIFFERENT MAROON COMMUNITIES WITH MANY DIFFERENT LEADERS AND THIS WAS THE HYDRA THE DUTCH TRIED TO SLAY AGAIN AND AGAIN.
SIMILAR MAROON COMMUNITIES DEVELOPED IN JAMAICA. ONE OF THEIR MOST RESPECTED LEADERS WAS A WOMAN CALLED GRANNY NANNY. A TOWN WAS NAMED AFTER HER, NANNY TOWN!
IN JAMAICA, THE BRITISH TRIED TO MAKE TREATIES WITH MAROONS, TO GET THEM TO STOP WELCOMING ESCAPEES INTO THEIR TOWNS.
SOME MAROONS WERE EVEN RECRUITED TO HUNT DOWN ESCAPED SLAVES.
IN SUCH CIRCUMSTANCES, THE DECENTRALIZED STRUCTURE OF THE MAROON MOVEMENT WAS AN ASSET. NO ONE LEADER SPOKE FOR ALL MAROONS SO IF ONE WAS BOUGHT OFF, OTHERS CONTINUED THE STRUGGLE.
SOME FIERCELY INDEPENDENT MAROON COMMUNITIES SURVIVE TO THIS DAY.

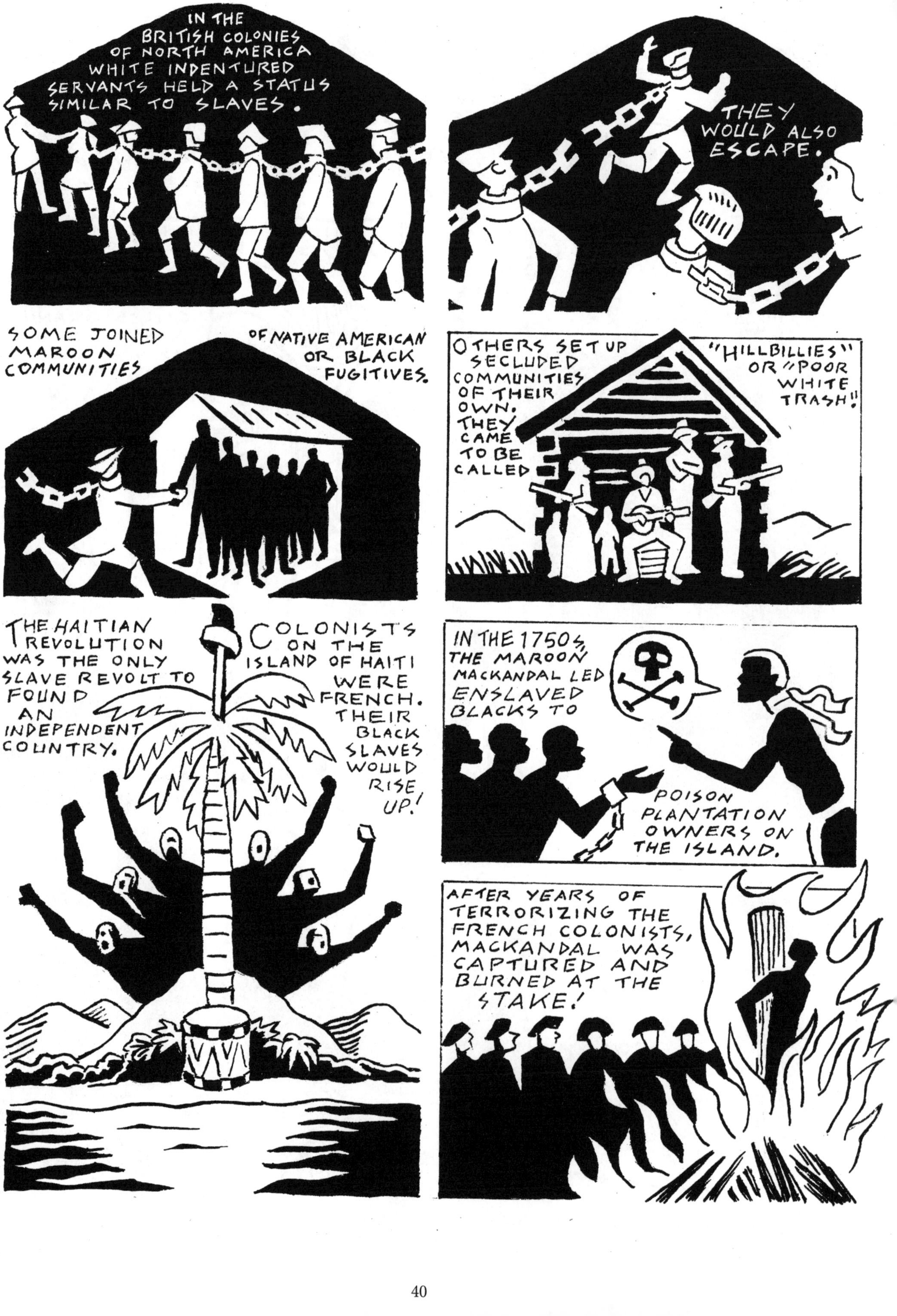
IN THE BRITISH COLONIES OF NORTH AMERICA WHITE INDENTURED SERVANTS HELD A STATUS SIMILAR TO SLAVES.
THEY WOULD ALSO ESCAPE.
SOME JOINED MAROON COMMUNITIES
OF NATIVE AMERICAN OR BLACK FUGITIVES.
OTHERS SET UP SECLUDED COMMUNITIES OF THEIR OWN. THEY CAME TO BE CALLED
"HILLBILLIES" OR "POOR WHITE TRASH!"
THE HAITIAN REVOLUTION WAS THE ONLY SLAVE REVOLT TO FOUND AN INDEPENDENT COUNTRY.
COLONISTS ON THE ISLAND OF HAITI WERE FRENCH. THEIR BLACK SLAVES WOULD RISE UP!
IN THE 1750s, THE MAROON MACKANDAL LED ENSLAVED BLACKS TO
POISON PLANTATION OWNERS ON THE ISLAND.
AFTER YEARS OF TERRORIZING THE FRENCH COLONISTS, MACKANDAL WAS CAPTURED AND BURNED AT THE STAKE!

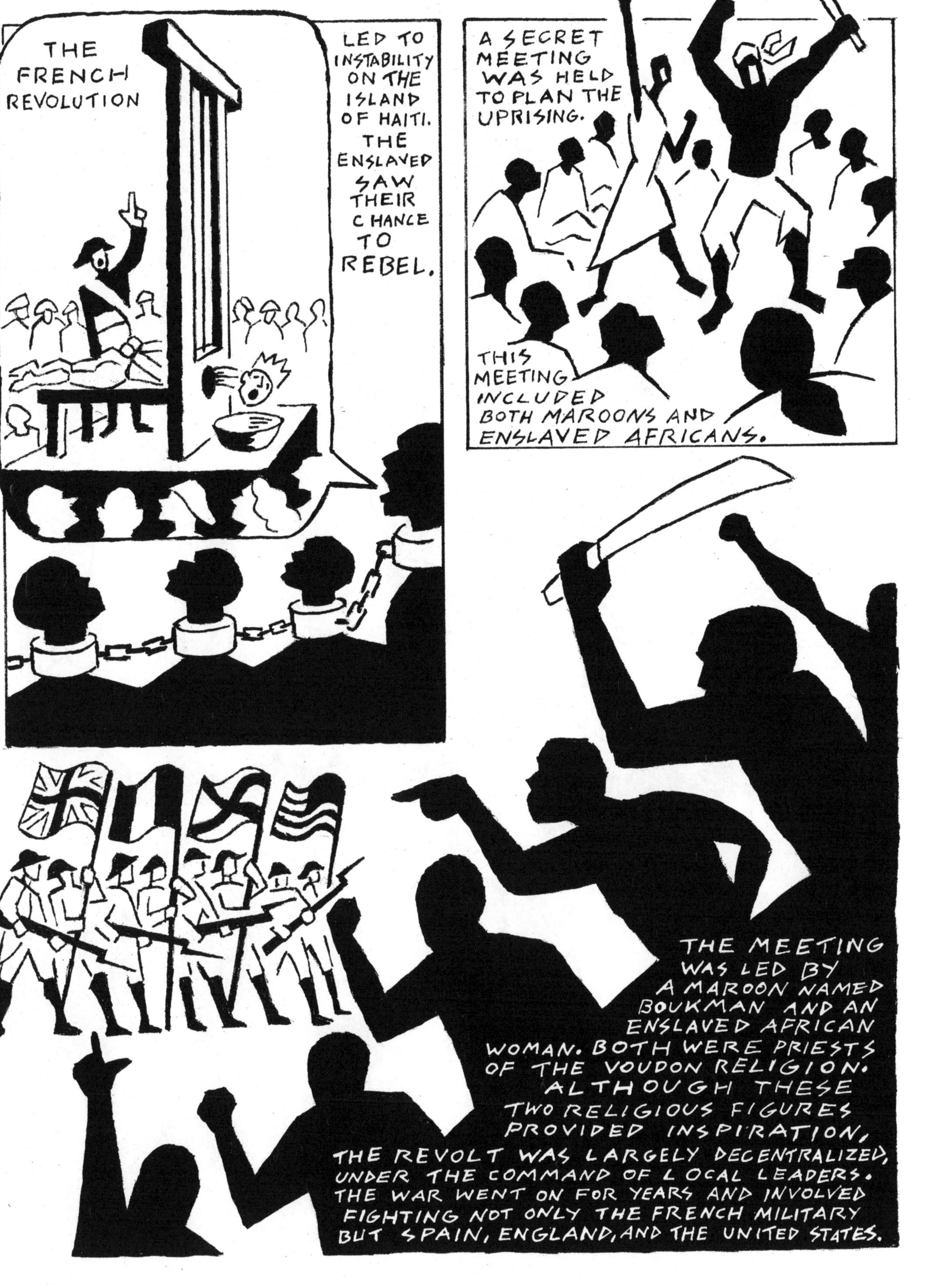
THE FRENCH REVOLUTION
LED TO INSTABILITY ON THE ISLAND OF HAITI. THE ENSLAVED SAW THEIR CHANCE TO REBEL.
A SECRET MEETING WAS HELD TO PLAN THE UPRISING.
THIS MEETING INCLUDED BOTH MAROONS AND ENSLAVED AFRICANS.
THE MEETING WAS LED BY A MAROON NAMED BOUKMAN AND AN ENSLAVED AFRICAN WOMAN. BOTH WERE PRIESTS OF THE VOUDON RELIGION. ALTHOUGH THESE TWO RELIGIOUS FIGURES PROVIDED INSPIRATION, THE REVOLT WAS LARGELY DECENTRALIZED, UNDER THE COMMAND OF LOCAL LEADERS. THE WAR WENT ON FOR YEARS AND INVOLVED FIGHTING NOT ONLY THE FRENCH MILITARY BUT SPAIN, ENGLAND, AND THE UNITED STATES.

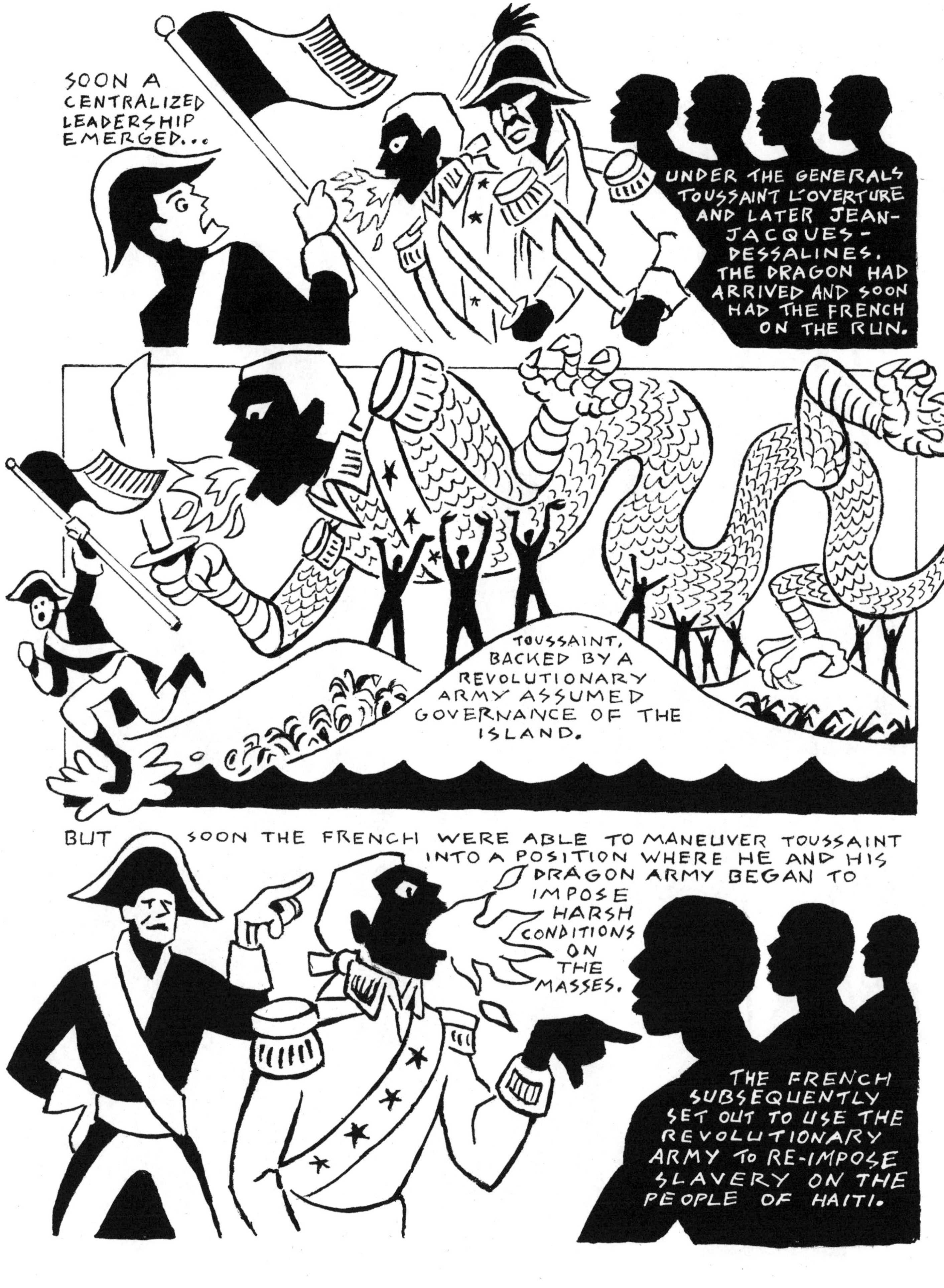
SOON A CENTRALIZED LEADERSHIP EMERGED...
UNDER THE GENERALS TOUSSAINT L'OVERTURE AND LATER JEAN-JACQUES-DESSALINES. THE DRAGON HAD ARRIVED AND SOON HAD THE FRENCH ON THE RUN.
TOUSSAINT, BACKED BY A REVOLUTIONARY ARMY ASSUMED GOVERNANCE OF THE ISLAND.
BUT SOON THE FRENCH WERE ABLE TO MANEUVER TOUSSAINT INTO A POSITION WHERE HE AND HIS DRAGON ARMY BEGAN TO IMPOSE HARSH CONDITIONS ON THE MASSES.
THE FRENCH SUBSEQUENTLY SET OUT TO USE THE REVOLUTIONARY ARMY TO RE-IMPOSE SLAVERY ON THE PEOPLE OF HAITI.

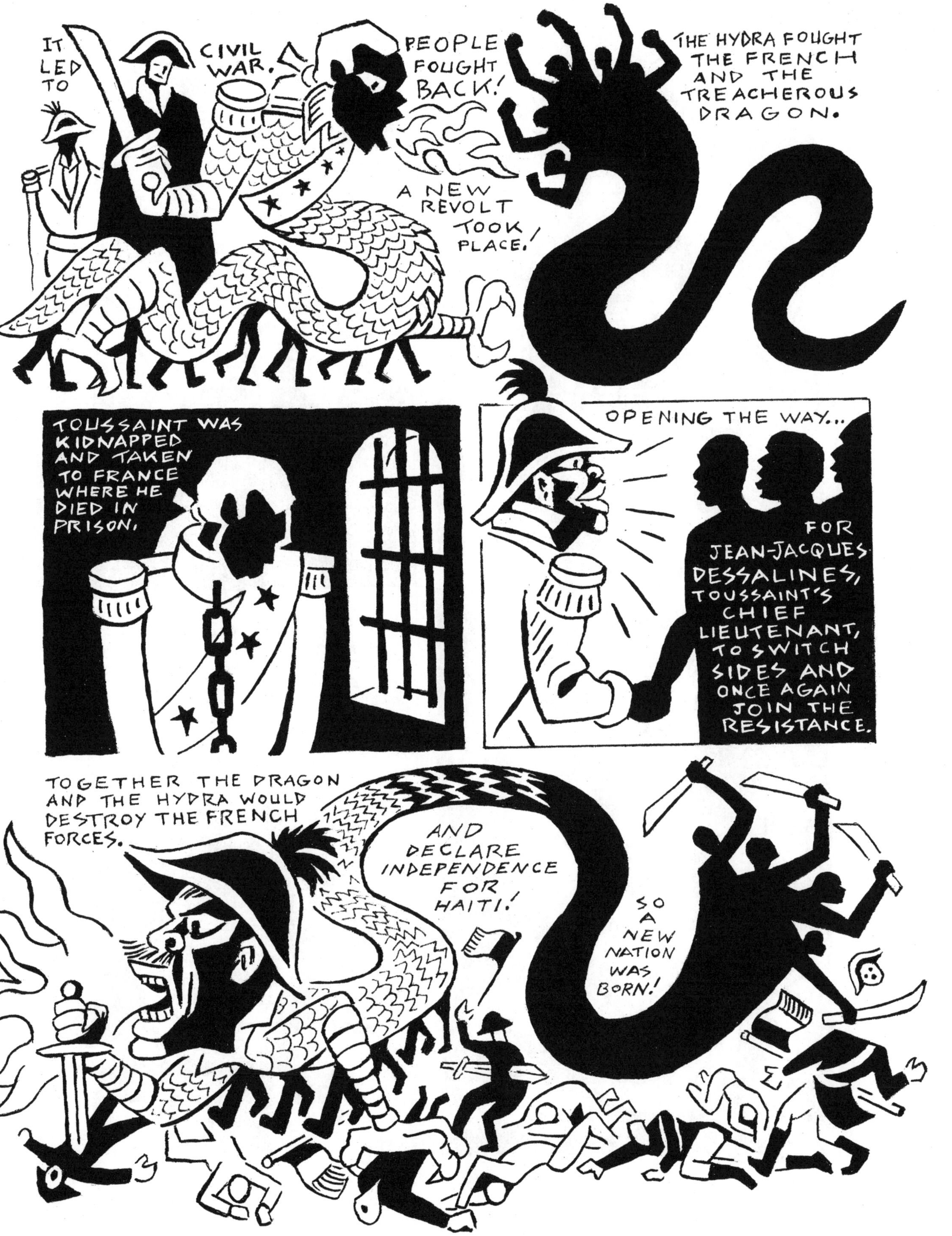
IT LED TO
CIVIL WAR.
PEOPLE FOUGHT BACK!
THE HYDRA FOUGHT THE FRENCH AND THE TREACHEROUS DRAGON.
A NEW REVOLT TOOK PLACE!
TOUSSAINT WAS KIDNAPPED AND TAKEN TO FRANCE WHERE HE DIED IN PRISON,
OPENING THE WAY...
FOR JEAN-JACQUES DESSALINES, TOUSSAINT'S CHIEF LIEUTENANT, TO SWITCH SIDES AND ONCE AGAIN JOIN THE RESISTANCE.
TOGETHER THE DRAGON AND THE HYDRA WOULD DESTROY THE FRENCH FORCES.
AND DECLARE INDEPENDENCE FOR HAITI!
SO A NEW NATION WAS BORN!

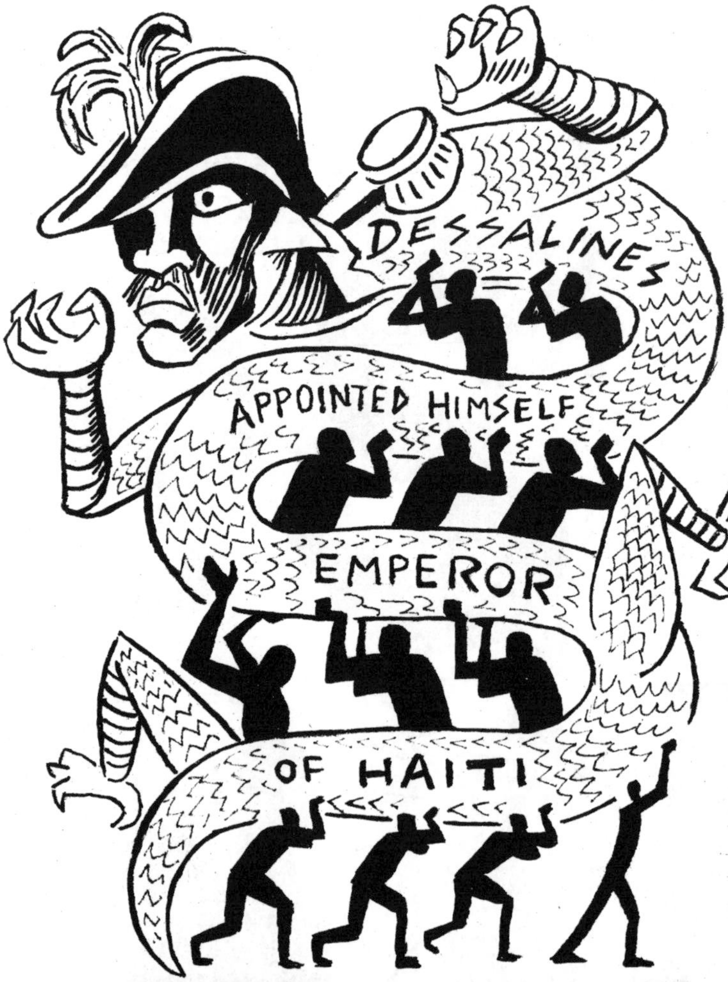
DESSALINES
APPOINTED HIMSELF
EMPEROR
OF HAITI

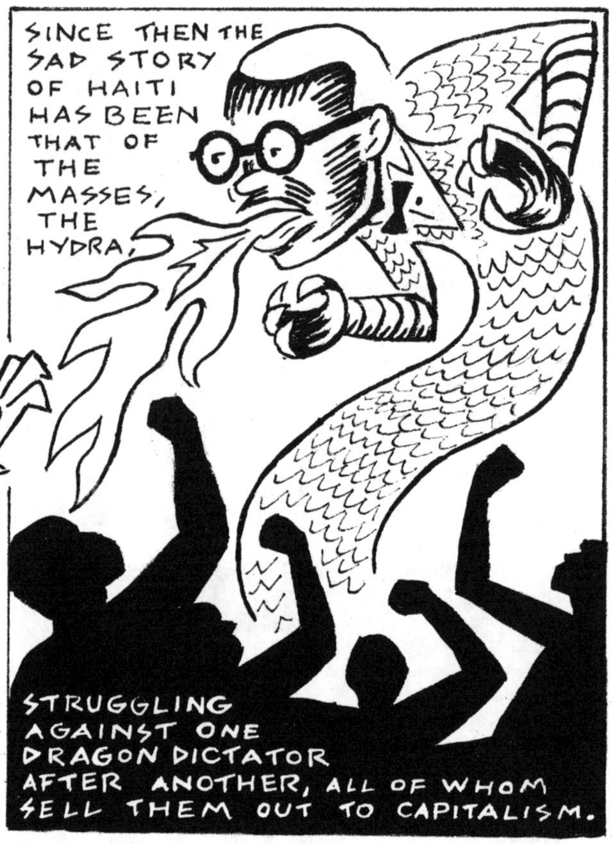
SINCE THEN THE SAD STORY OF HAITI HAS BEEN THAT OF THE MASSES, THE HYDRA,
STRUGGLING AGAINST ONE DRAGON DICTATOR AFTER ANOTHER, ALL OF WHOM SELL THEM OUT TO CAPITALISM.

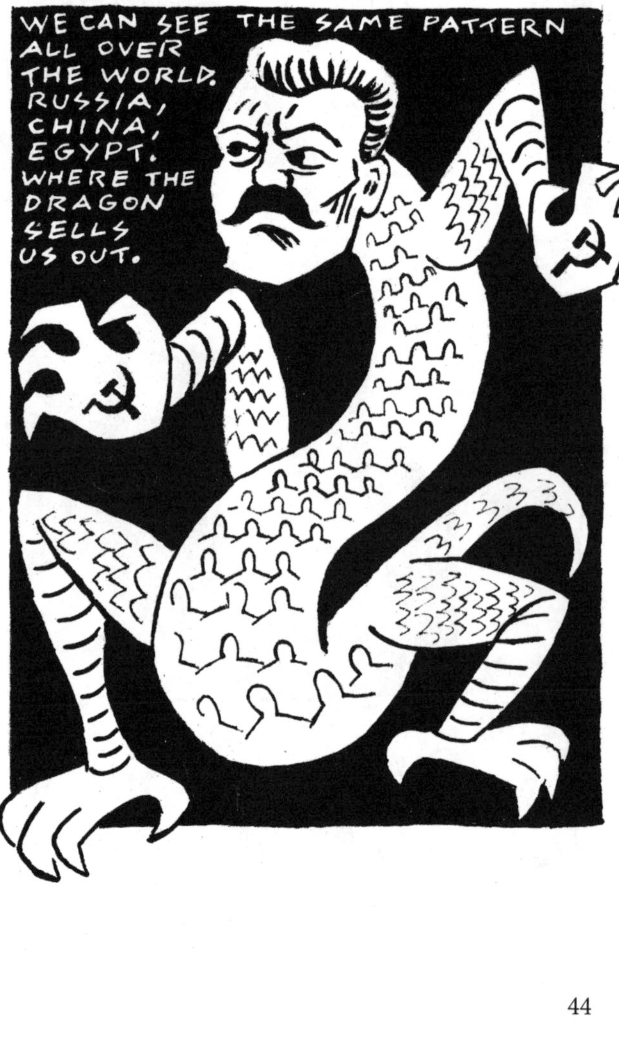
WE CAN SEE THE SAME PATTERN ALL OVER THE WORLD. RUSSIA, CHINA, EGYPT. WHERE THE DRAGON SELLS US OUT.

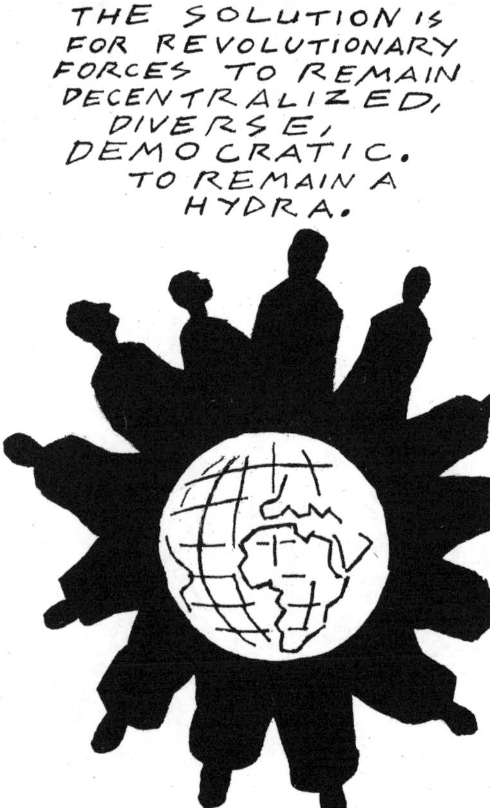
THE SOLUTION IS FOR REVOLUTIONARY FORCES TO REMAIN DECENTRALIZED, DIVERSE, DEMOCRATIC. TO REMAIN A HYDRA.

MAYBE A MOSAIC IS A BETTER METAPHOR. WE ARE A

Movement of
Oppressed
Sectors
Acting
In
Concert.

A MOSAIC IS A WORK OF ART MADE BY ASSEMBLING MANY COLORED TILES INTO ONE DESIGN. PIECES RETAIN THEIR IDENTITY. THE ARTIST DOES NOT CHANGE THEM.

A MOVEMENT OF THE 21ST CENTURY WILL BE AN ASSEMBLY OF MANY COMMUNITIES INCLUDING: WOMEN, NEW AFRIKAN & PAN-AFRIKAN PEOPLES, PUERTO RICANS, ANARCHISTS, ASIANS, CHICANOS & MEXICANS, NATIVE AMERICANS, EURO-AMERICANS, LESBIAN, GAY, BISEXUAL, TRANSGENDER AND GENDERQUEER PEOPLE, ECOLOGICAL ACTIVISTS, ANIMAL RIGHTS ACTIVISTS, WORKING-CLASS PEOPLE, PEOPLE WITH DISABILITIES, PEOPLE WHO HAVE BEEN INCARCERATED, AND MANY OTHERS!

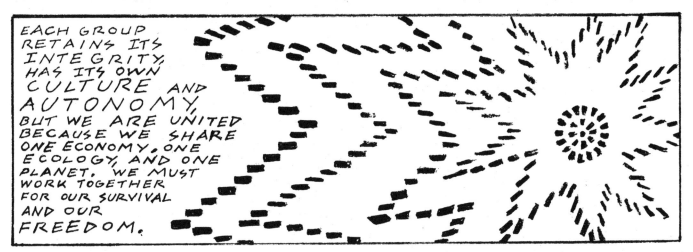

EACH GROUP RETAINS ITS INTEGRITY. HAS ITS OWN CULTURE AND AUTONOMY, BUT WE ARE UNITED BECAUSE WE SHARE ONE ECONOMY, ONE ECOLOGY, AND ONE PLANET. WE MUST WORK TOGETHER FOR OUR SURVIVAL AND OUR FREEDOM.

Modern Maroons

illustrated by Hannah Allen, Emmy Kepler, and Songe Riddle

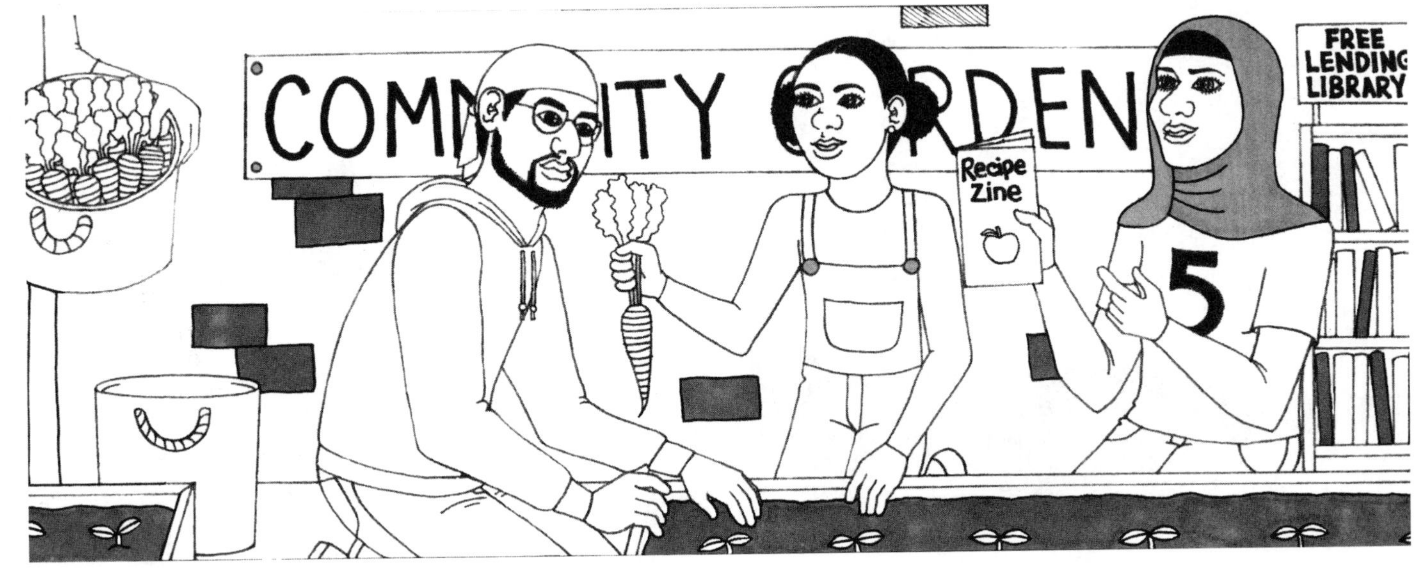

COMM ITY RDEN
FREE LENDING LIBRARY
Recipe Zine
5

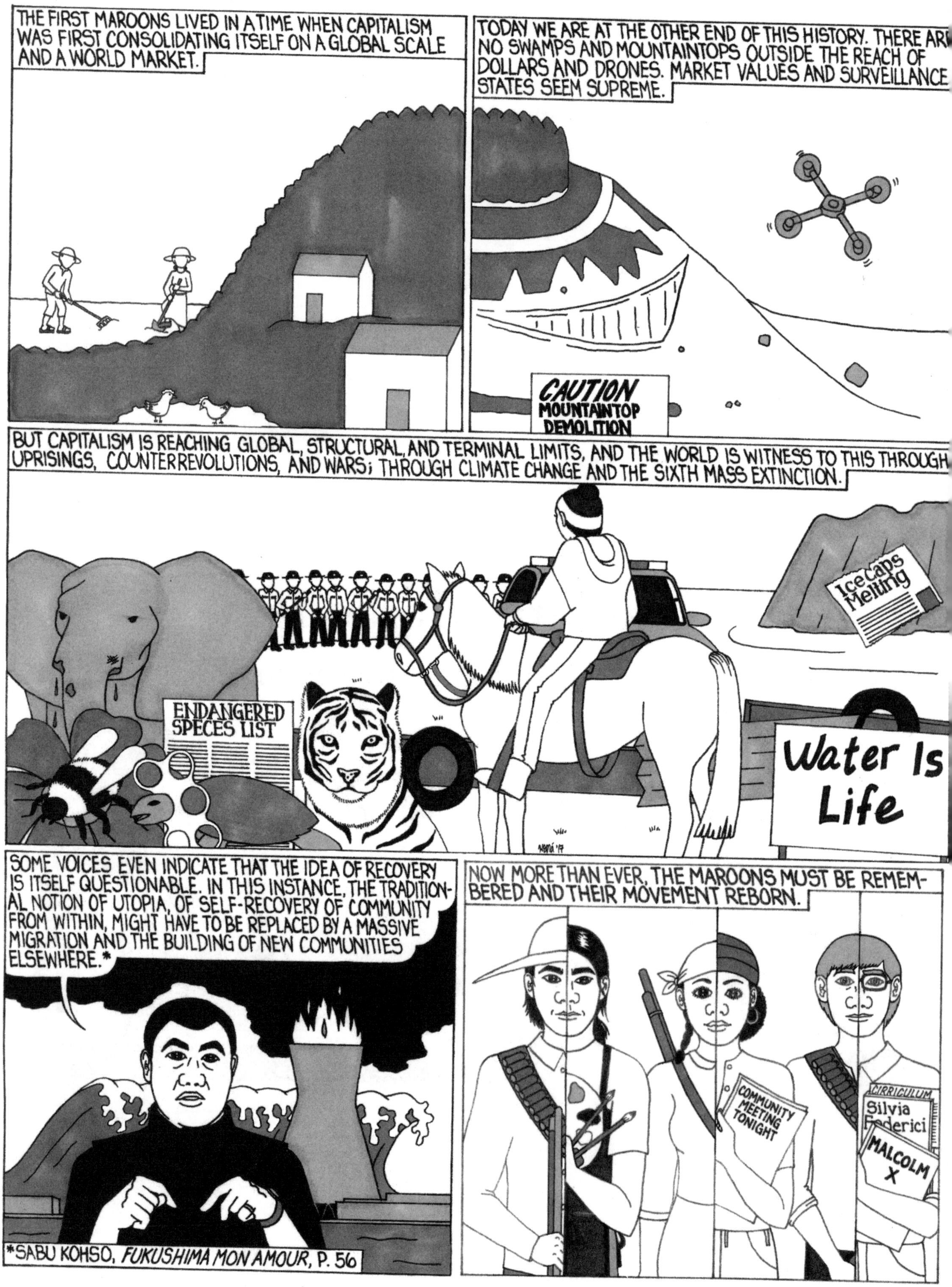
THE FIRST MAROONS LIVED IN A TIME WHEN CAPITALISM WAS FIRST CONSOLIDATING ITSELF ON A GLOBAL SCALE AND A WORLD MARKET.
TODAY WE ARE AT THE OTHER END OF THIS HISTORY. THERE AR NO SWAMPS AND MOUNTAINTOPS OUTSIDE THE REACH OF DOLLARS AND DRONES. MARKET VALUES AND SURVEILLANCE STATES SEEM SUPREME.
CAUTION
MOUNTAINTOP
DEMOLITION
BUT CAPITALISM IS REACHING GLOBAL, STRUCTURAL, AND TERMINAL LIMITS, AND THE WORLD IS WITNESS TO THIS THROUGH UPRISINGS, COUNTERREVOLUTIONS, AND WARS; THROUGH CLIMATE CHANGE AND THE SIXTH MASS EXTINCTION.
Icecaps Melting
ENDANGERED SPECIES LIST
Water Is Life
SOME VOICES EVEN INDICATE THAT THE IDEA OF RECOVERY IS ITSELF QUESTIONABLE. IN THIS INSTANCE, THE TRADITIONAL NOTION OF UTOPIA, OF SELF-RECOVERY OF COMMUNITY FROM WITHIN, MIGHT HAVE TO BE REPLACED BY A MASSIVE MIGRATION AND THE BUILDING OF NEW COMMUNITIES ELSEWHERE.*
*SABU KOHSO, FUKUSHIMA MON AMOUR, P. 56
NOW MORE THAN EVER, THE MAROONS MUST BE REMEMBERED AND THEIR MOVEMENT REBORN.
COMMUNITY MEETING TONIGHT
CIRRICULUM
Silvia Federici
MALCOLM X

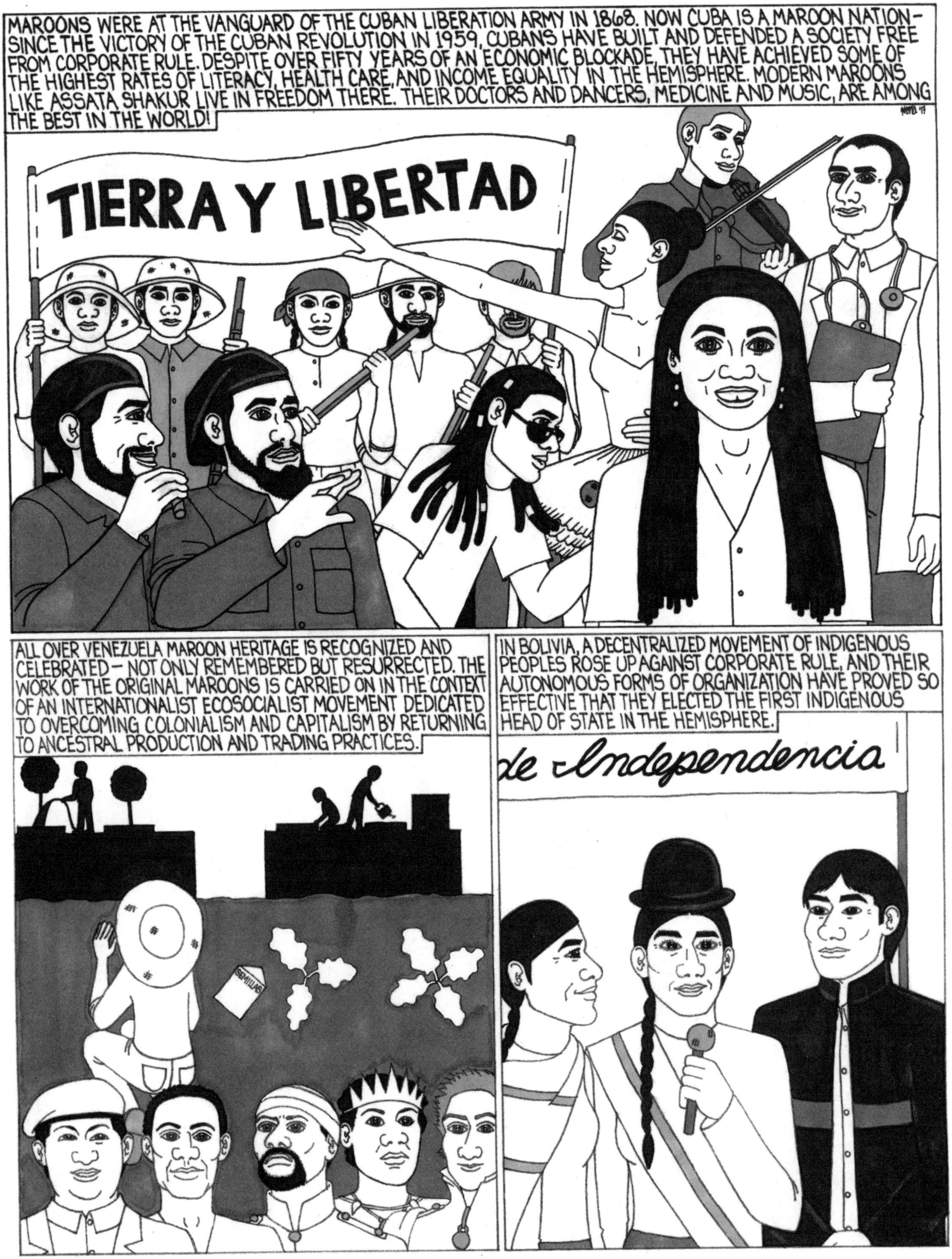
MAROONS WERE AT THE VANGUARD OF THE CUBAN LIBERATION ARMY IN 1868. NOW CUBA IS A MAROON NATION– SINCE THE VICTORY OF THE CUBAN REVOLUTION IN 1959, CUBANS HAVE BUILT AND DEFENDED A SOCIETY FREE FROM CORPORATE RULE. DESPITE OVER FIFTY YEARS OF AN ECONOMIC BLOCKADE, THEY HAVE ACHIEVED SOME OF THE HIGHEST RATES OF LITERACY, HEALTH CARE, AND INCOME EQUALITY IN THE HEMISPHERE. MODERN MAROONS LIKE ASSATA SHAKUR LIVE IN FREEDOM THERE. THEIR DOCTORS AND DANCERS, MEDICINE AND MUSIC, ARE AMONG THE BEST IN THE WORLD!
TIERRA Y LIBERTAD
ALL OVER VENEZUELA MAROON HERITAGE IS RECOGNIZED AND CELEBRATED– NOT ONLY REMEMBERED BUT RESURRECTED. THE WORK OF THE ORIGINAL MAROONS IS CARRIED ON IN THE CONTEXT OF AN INTERNATIONALIST ECOSOCIALIST MOVEMENT DEDICATED TO OVERCOMING COLONIALISM AND CAPITALISM BY RETURNING TO ANCESTRAL PRODUCTION AND TRADING PRACTICES.
SEMILLAS
IN BOLIVIA, A DECENTRALIZED MOVEMENT OF INDIGENOUS PEOPLES ROSE UP AGAINST CORPORATE RULE, AND THEIR AUTONOMOUS FORMS OF ORGANIZATION HAVE PROVED SO EFFECTIVE THAT THEY ELECTED THE FIRST INDIGENOUS HEAD OF STATE IN THE HEMISPHERE.
de Independencia

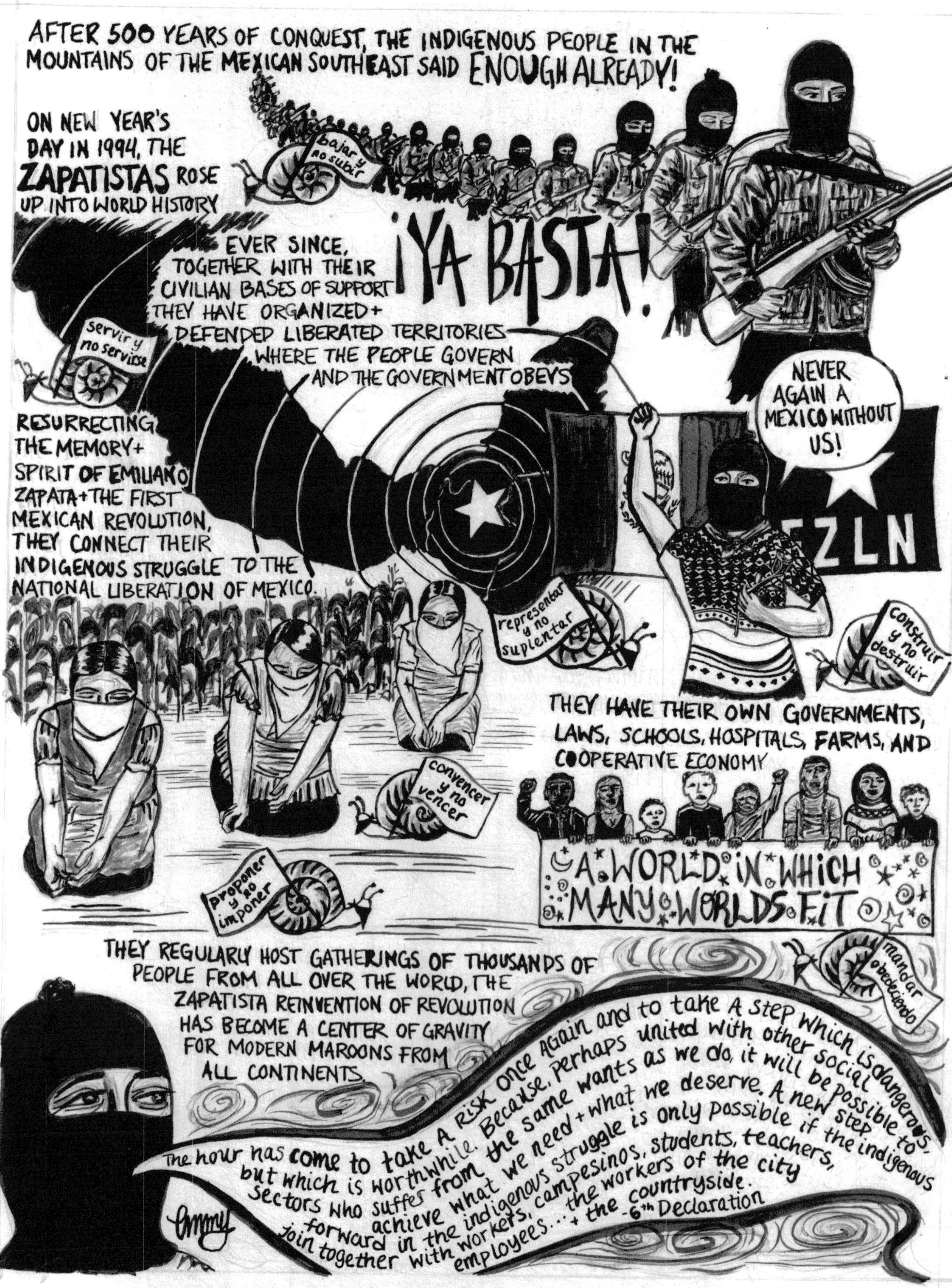

AFTER 500 YEARS OF CONQUEST, THE INDIGENOUS PEOPLE IN THE MOUNTAINS OF THE MEXICAN SOUTHEAST SAID ENOUGH ALREADY!
ON NEW YEAR'S DAY IN 1994, THE ZAPATISTAS ROSE UP INTO WORLD HISTORY
bajar y no subir
¡YA BASTA!
EVER SINCE, TOGETHER WITH THEIR CIVILIAN BASES OF SUPPORT THEY HAVE ORGANIZED + DEFENDED LIBERATED TERRITORIES WHERE THE PEOPLE GOVERN AND THE GOVERNMENT OBEYS
servir y no servirse
NEVER AGAIN A MEXICO WITHOUT US!
RESURRECTING THE MEMORY + SPIRIT OF EMILIANO ZAPATA + THE FIRST MEXICAN REVOLUTION, THEY CONNECT THEIR INDIGENOUS STRUGGLE TO THE NATIONAL LIBERATION OF MEXICO.
EZLN
representar y no suplantar
construir y no destruir
THEY HAVE THEIR OWN GOVERNMENTS, LAWS, SCHOOLS, HOSPITALS, FARMS, AND COOPERATIVE ECONOMY
convencer y no vencer
A WORLD IN WHICH MANY WORLDS FIT
proponer y no imponer
mandar obedeciendo
THEY REGULARLY HOST GATHERINGS OF THOUSANDS OF PEOPLE FROM ALL OVER THE WORLD, THE ZAPATISTA REINVENTION OF REVOLUTION HAS BECOME A CENTER OF GRAVITY FOR MODERN MAROONS FROM ALL CONTINENTS.
The hour has come to take a risk once again and to take a step which is dangerous, but which is worthwhile. Because, perhaps united with other social sectors who suffer from the same wants as we do, it will be possible to achieve what we need + what we deserve. A new step forward in the indigenous struggle is only possible if the indigenous join together with workers, campesinos, students, teachers, employees... + the workers of the city + the countryside. -6th Declaration
Emmy

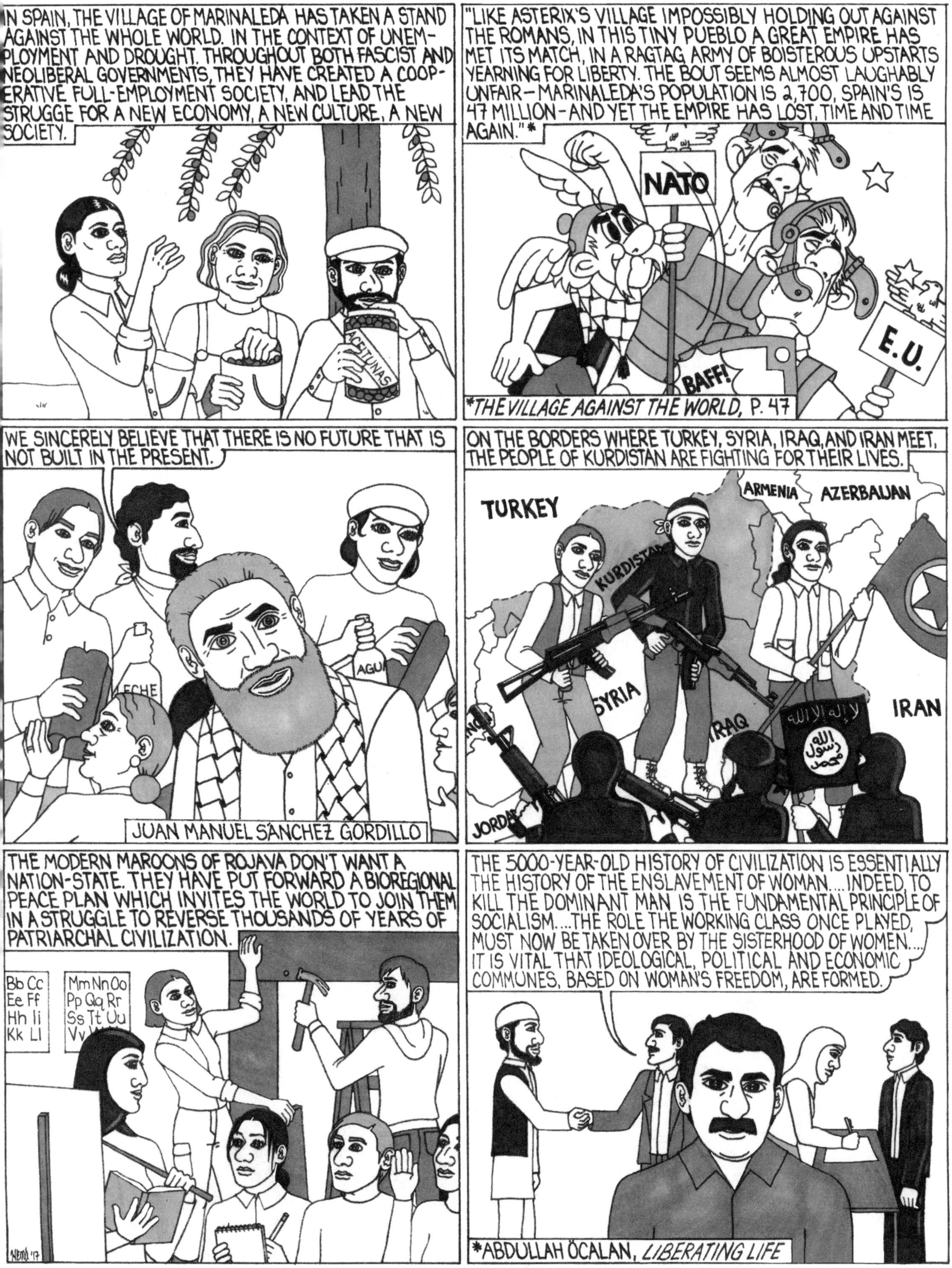
IN SPAIN, THE VILLAGE OF MARINALEDA HAS TAKEN A STAND AGAINST THE WHOLE WORLD. IN THE CONTEXT OF UNEMPLOYMENT AND DROUGHT, THROUGHOUT BOTH FASCIST AND NEOLIBERAL GOVERNMENTS, THEY HAVE CREATED A COOPERATIVE FULL-EMPLOYMENT SOCIETY, AND LEAD THE STRUGGE FOR A NEW ECONOMY, A NEW CULTURE, A NEW SOCIETY.
ACEITUNAS
"LIKE ASTERIX'S VILLAGE IMPOSSIBLY HOLDING OUT AGAINST THE ROMANS, IN THIS TINY PUEBLO A GREAT EMPIRE HAS MET ITS MATCH, IN A RAGTAG ARMY OF BOISTEROUS UPSTARTS YEARNING FOR LIBERTY. THE BOUT SEEMS ALMOST LAUGHABLY UNFAIR—MARINALEDA'S POPULATION IS 2,700, SPAIN'S IS 47 MILLION—AND YET THE EMPIRE HAS LOST, TIME AND TIME AGAIN." *
NATO
E.U.
BAFF!
*THE VILLAGE AGAINST THE WORLD, P. 47
WE SINCERELY BELIEVE THAT THERE IS NO FUTURE THAT IS NOT BUILT IN THE PRESENT.
JUAN MANUEL SÁNCHEZ GORDILLO
ON THE BORDERS WHERE TURKEY, SYRIA, IRAQ, AND IRAN MEET, THE PEOPLE OF KURDISTAN ARE FIGHTING FOR THEIR LIVES.
TURKEY
ARMENIA
AZERBAIJAN
KURDISTAN
SYRIA
IRAQ
IRAN
THE MODERN MAROONS OF ROJAVA DON'T WANT A NATION-STATE. THEY HAVE PUT FORWARD A BIOREGIONAL PEACE PLAN WHICH INVITES THE WORLD TO JOIN THEM IN A STRUGGLE TO REVERSE THOUSANDS OF YEARS OF PATRIARCHAL CIVILIZATION.
Bb Cc Ee Ff Hh Ii Kk Ll
Mm Nn Oo Pp Qq Rr Ss Tt Uu
THE 5000-YEAR-OLD HISTORY OF CIVILIZATION IS ESSENTIALLY THE HISTORY OF THE ENSLAVEMENT OF WOMAN.... INDEED, TO KILL THE DOMINANT MAN IS THE FUNDAMENTAL PRINCIPLE OF SOCIALISM.... THE ROLE THE WORKING CLASS ONCE PLAYED, MUST NOW BE TAKEN OVER BY THE SISTERHOOD OF WOMEN.... IT IS VITAL THAT IDEOLOGICAL, POLITICAL AND ECONOMIC COMMUNES, BASED ON WOMAN'S FREEDOM, ARE FORMED.
*ABDULLAH ÖCALAN, LIBERATING LIFE

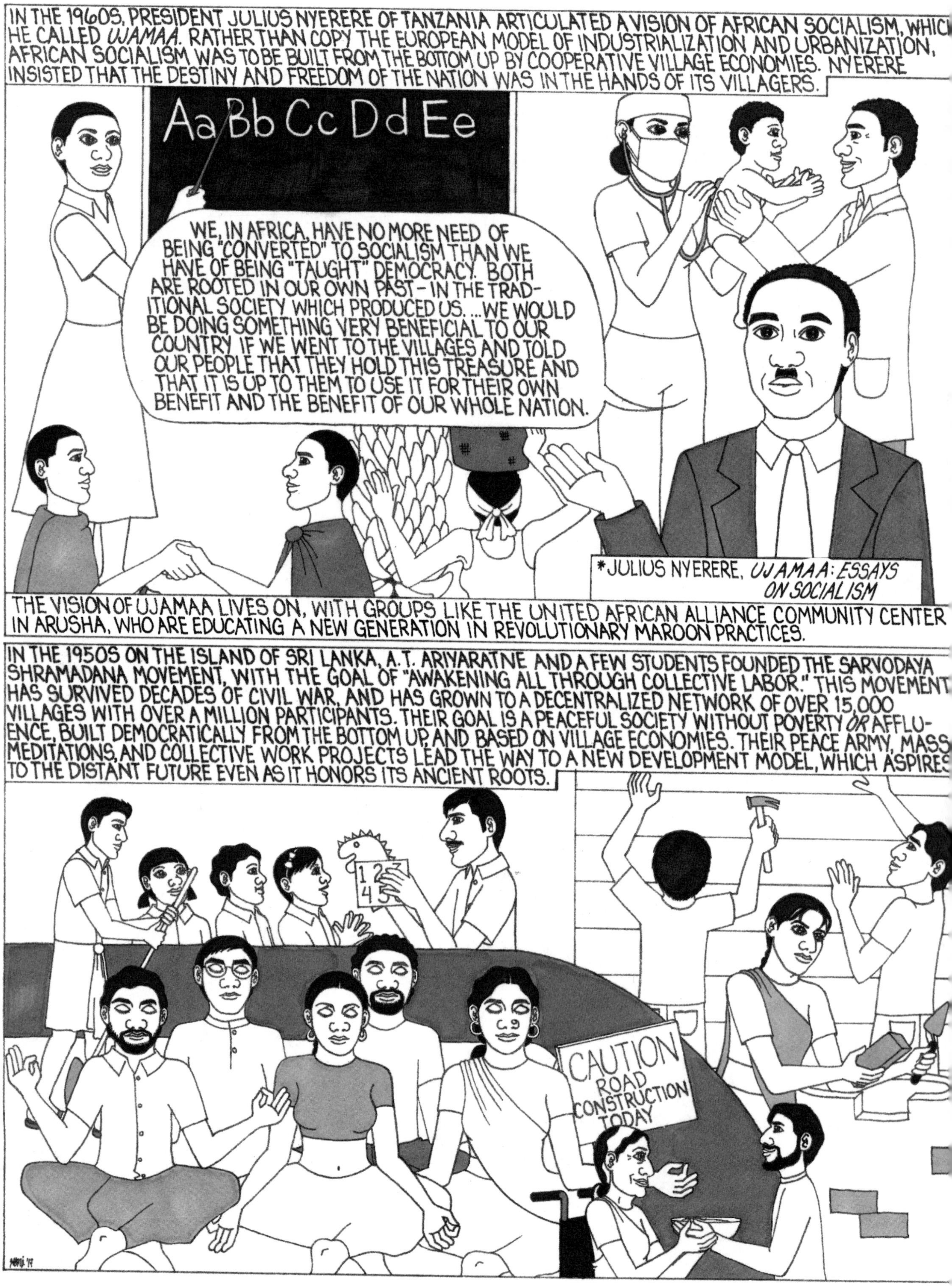
IN THE 1960S, PRESIDENT JULIUS NYERERE OF TANZANIA ARTICULATED A VISION OF AFRICAN SOCIALISM, WHIC
HE CALLED *UJAMAA*. RATHER THAN COPY THE EUROPEAN MODEL OF INDUSTRIALIZATION AND URBANIZATION, AFRICAN SOCIALISM WAS TO BE BUILT FROM THE BOTTOM UP BY COOPERATIVE VILLAGE ECONOMIES. NYERERE INSISTED THAT THE DESTINY AND FREEDOM OF THE NATION WAS IN THE HANDS OF ITS VILLAGERS.
Aa Bb Cc Dd Ee
WE, IN AFRICA, HAVE NO MORE NEED OF BEING "CONVERTED" TO SOCIALISM THAN WE HAVE OF BEING "TAUGHT" DEMOCRACY. BOTH ARE ROOTED IN OUR OWN PAST – IN THE TRADITIONAL SOCIETY WHICH PRODUCED US. ... WE WOULD BE DOING SOMETHING VERY BENEFICIAL TO OUR COUNTRY IF WE WENT TO THE VILLAGES AND TOLD OUR PEOPLE THAT THEY HOLD THIS TREASURE AND THAT IT IS UP TO THEM TO USE IT FOR THEIR OWN BENEFIT AND THE BENEFIT OF OUR WHOLE NATION.
*JULIUS NYERERE, *UJAMAA: ESSAYS ON SOCIALISM*
THE VISION OF UJAMAA LIVES ON, WITH GROUPS LIKE THE UNITED AFRICAN ALLIANCE COMMUNITY CENTER IN ARUSHA, WHO ARE EDUCATING A NEW GENERATION IN REVOLUTIONARY MAROON PRACTICES.
IN THE 1950S ON THE ISLAND OF SRI LANKA, A.T. ARIYARATNE AND A FEW STUDENTS FOUNDED THE SARVODAYA SHRAMADANA MOVEMENT, WITH THE GOAL OF "AWAKENING ALL THROUGH COLLECTIVE LABOR." THIS MOVEMENT HAS SURVIVED DECADES OF CIVIL WAR, AND HAS GROWN TO A DECENTRALIZED NETWORK OF OVER 15,000 VILLAGES WITH OVER A MILLION PARTICIPANTS. THEIR GOAL IS A PEACEFUL SOCIETY WITHOUT POVERTY *OR* AFFLUENCE, BUILT DEMOCRATICALLY FROM THE BOTTOM UP, AND BASED ON VILLAGE ECONOMIES. THEIR PEACE ARMY, MASS MEDITATIONS, AND COLLECTIVE WORK PROJECTS LEAD THE WAY TO A NEW DEVELOPMENT MODEL, WHICH ASPIRES TO THE DISTANT FUTURE EVEN AS IT HONORS ITS ANCIENT ROOTS.
1 2 3
4 5
CAUTION ROAD CONSTRUCTION TODAY

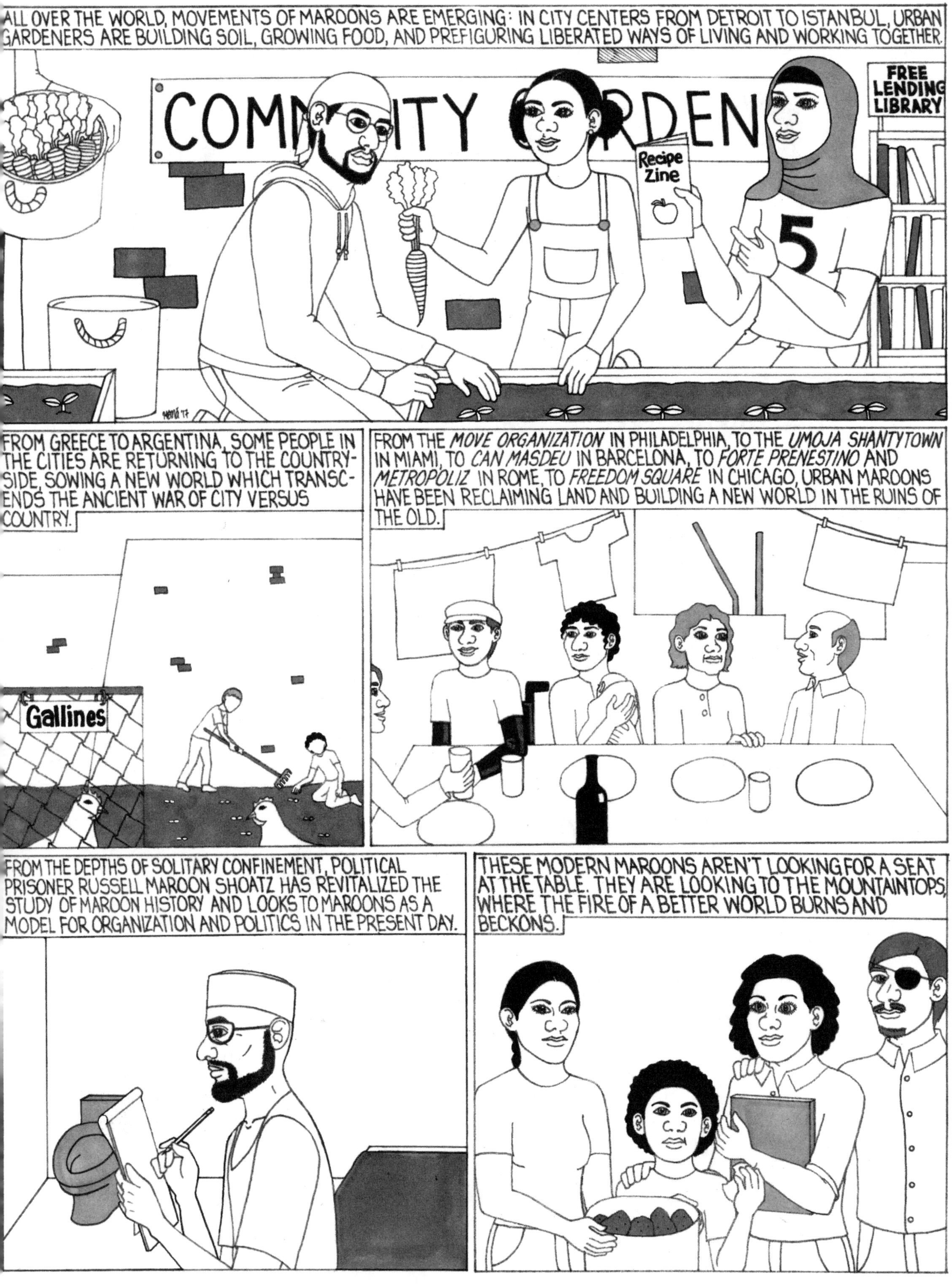
ALL OVER THE WORLD, MOVEMENTS OF MAROONS ARE EMERGING: IN CITY CENTERS FROM DETROIT TO ISTANBUL, URBAN GARDENERS ARE BUILDING SOIL, GROWING FOOD, AND PREFIGURING LIBERATED WAYS OF LIVING AND WORKING TOGETHER.
FREE LENDING LIBRARY
Recipe Zine
5
FROM GREECE TO ARGENTINA, SOME PEOPLE IN THE CITIES ARE RETURNING TO THE COUNTRYSIDE, SOWING A NEW WORLD WHICH TRANSCENDS THE ANCIENT WAR OF CITY VERSUS COUNTRY.
Gallines
FROM THE *MOVE ORGANIZATION* IN PHILADELPHIA, TO THE *UMOJA SHANTYTOWN* IN MIAMI, TO *CAN MASDEU* IN BARCELONA, TO *FORTE PRENESTINO* AND *METROPOLIZ* IN ROME, TO *FREEDOM SQUARE* IN CHICAGO, URBAN MAROONS HAVE BEEN RECLAIMING LAND AND BUILDING A NEW WORLD IN THE RUINS OF THE OLD.
FROM THE DEPTHS OF SOLITARY CONFINEMENT, POLITICAL PRISONER RUSSELL MAROON SHOATZ HAS REVITALIZED THE STUDY OF MAROON HISTORY AND LOOKS TO MAROONS AS A MODEL FOR ORGANIZATION AND POLITICS IN THE PRESENT DAY.
THESE MODERN MAROONS AREN'T LOOKING FOR A SEAT AT THE TABLE. THEY ARE LOOKING TO THE MOUNTAINTOPS, WHERE THE FIRE OF A BETTER WORLD BURNS AND BECKONS.

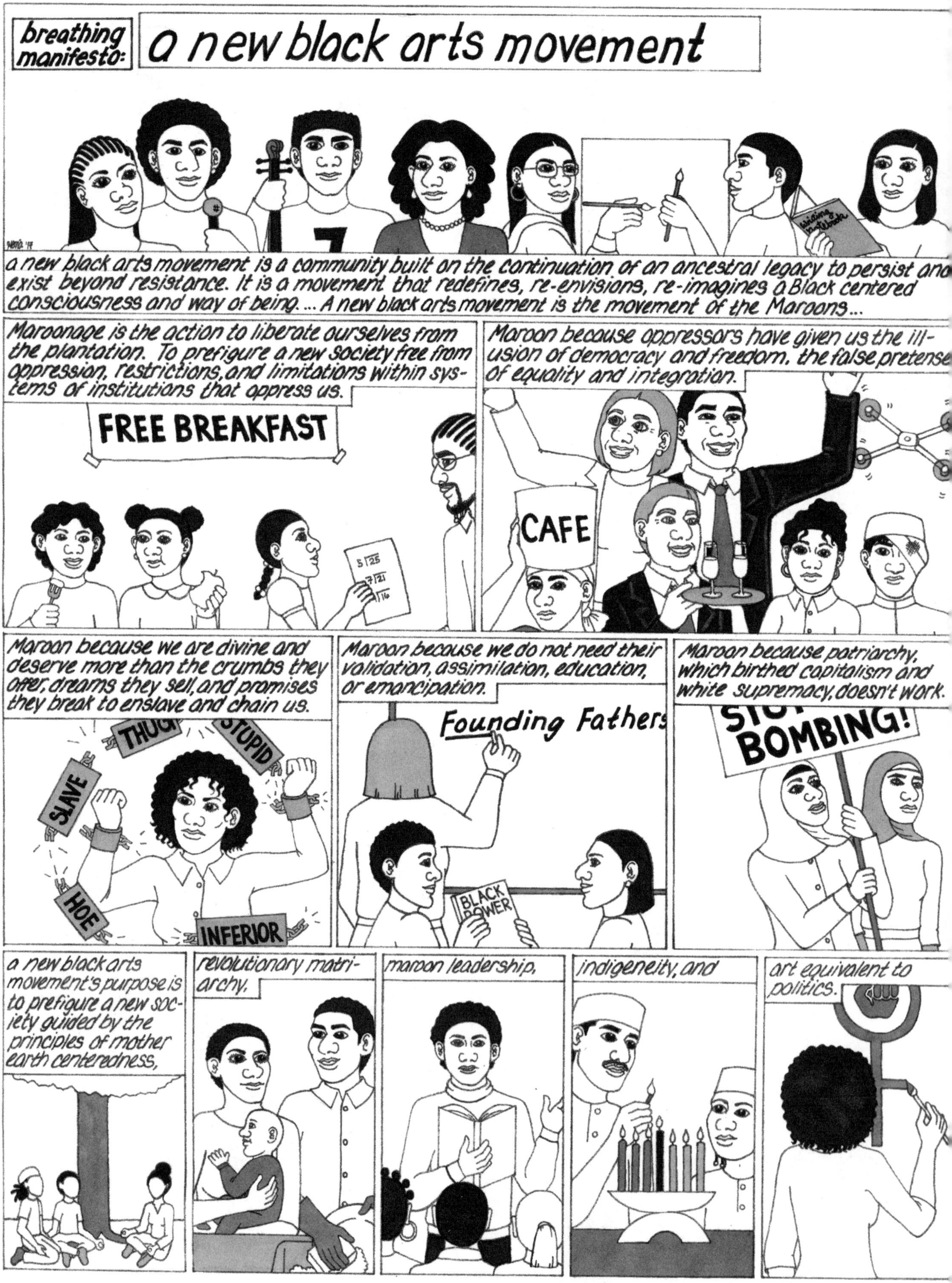

breathing manifesto:
a new black arts movement
a new black arts movement is a community built on the continuation of an ancestral legacy to persist and exist beyond resistance. It is a movement that redefines, re-envisions, re-imagines a Black centered consciousness and way of being.... A new black arts movement is the movement of the Maroons...
Maroonage is the action to liberate ourselves from the plantation. To prefigure a new society free from oppression, restrictions, and limitations within systems of institutions that oppress us.
FREE BREAKFAST
Maroon because oppressors have given us the illusion of democracy and freedom, the false pretense of equality and integration.
CAFE
Maroon because we are divine and deserve more than the crumbs they offer, dreams they sell, and promises they break to enslave and chain us.
THUG
STUPID
SLAVE
HOE
INFERIOR
Maroon because we do not need their validation, assimilation, education, or emancipation.
Founding Fathers
BLACK
Maroon because patriarchy, which birthed capitalism and white supremacy, doesn't work.
BOMBING!
a new black arts movement's purpose is to prefigure a new society guided by the principles of mother earth centeredness,
revolutionary matriarchy,
maroon leadership,
indigeneity, and
art equivalent to politics.

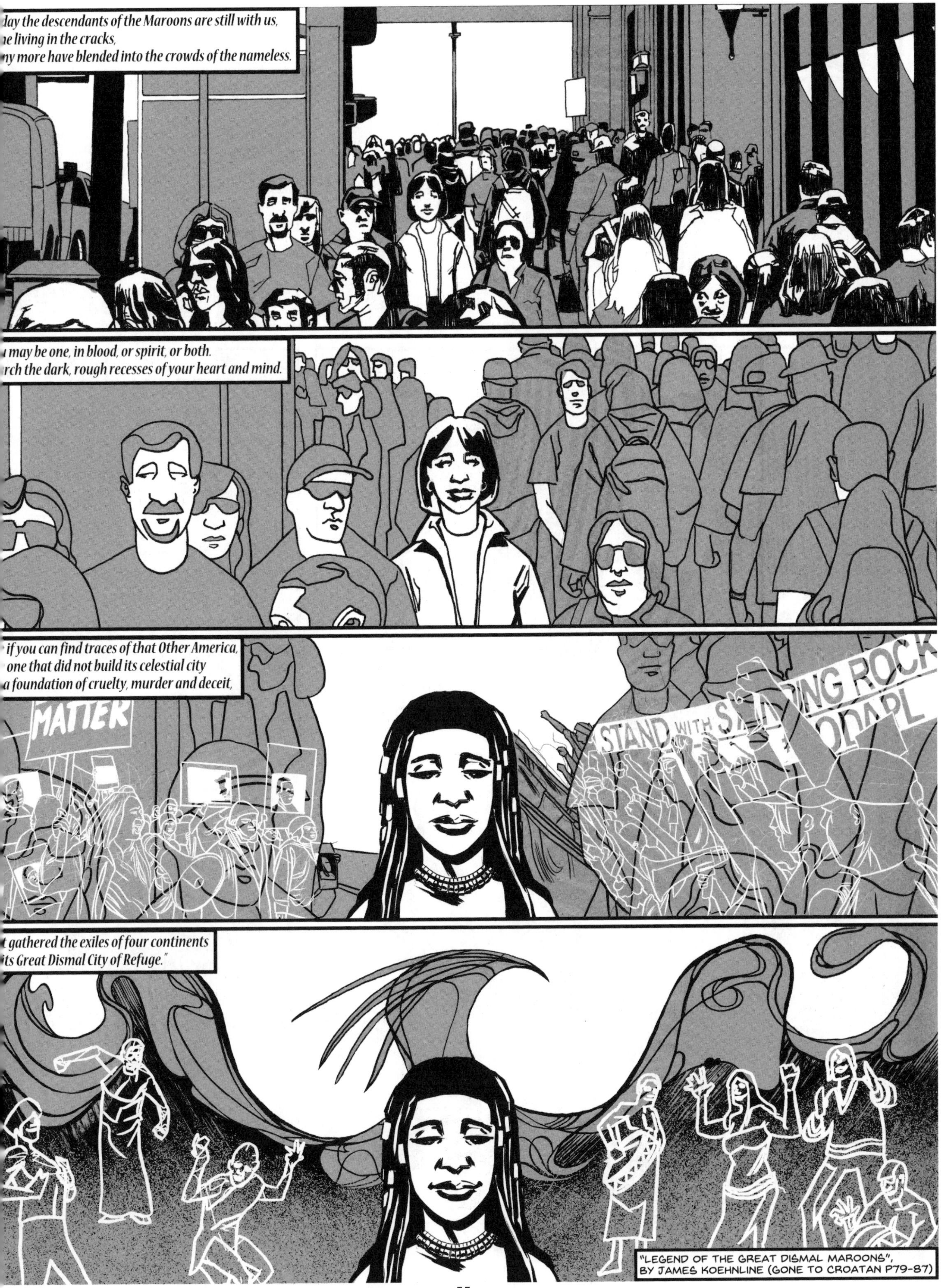
day the descendants of the Maroons are still with us,
ne living in the cracks,
ny more have blended into the crowds of the nameless.
may be one, in blood, or spirit, or both.
rch the dark, rough recesses of your heart and mind.
if you can find traces of that Other America,
one that did not build its celestial city
a foundation of cruelty, murder and deceit,
MATTER
STAND WITH
t gathered the exiles of four continents
its Great Dismal City of Refuge."
"LEGEND OF THE GREAT DISMAL MAROONS",
BY JAMES KOEHNLINE (GONE TO CROATAN P79-87)

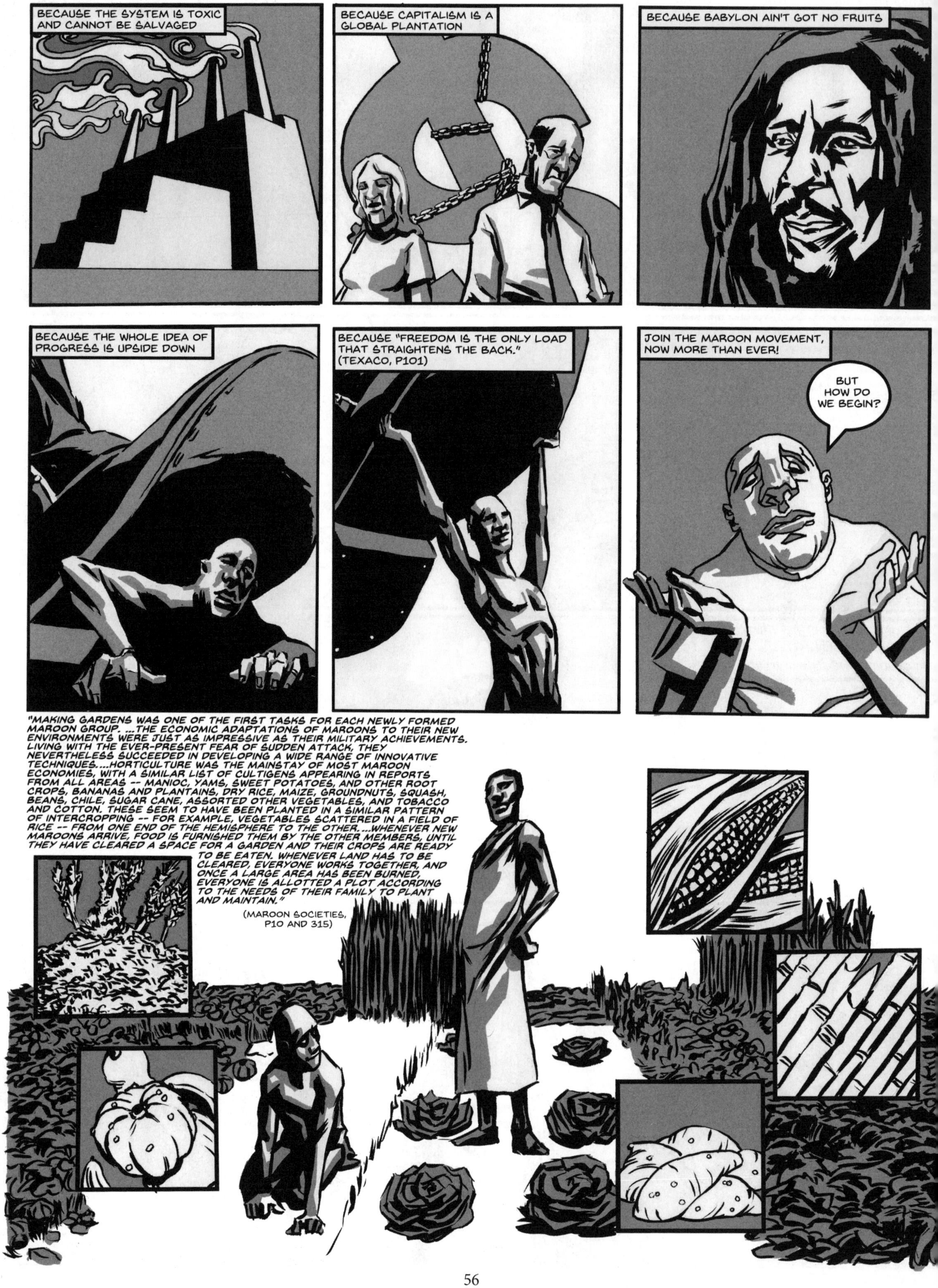

BECAUSE THE SYSTEM IS TOXIC AND CANNOT BE SALVAGED
BECAUSE CAPITALISM IS A GLOBAL PLANTATION
BECAUSE BABYLON AIN'T GOT NO FRUITS
BECAUSE THE WHOLE IDEA OF PROGRESS IS UPSIDE DOWN
BECAUSE "FREEDOM IS THE ONLY LOAD THAT STRAIGHTENS THE BACK." (TEXACO, P101)
JOIN THE MAROON MOVEMENT, NOW MORE THAN EVER!
BUT HOW DO WE BEGIN?
"MAKING GARDENS WAS ONE OF THE FIRST TASKS FOR EACH NEWLY FORMED MAROON GROUP. ...THE ECONOMIC ADAPTATIONS OF MAROONS TO THEIR NEW ENVIRONMENTS WERE JUST AS IMPRESSIVE AS THEIR MILITARY ACHIEVEMENTS. LIVING WITH THE EVER-PRESENT FEAR OF SUDDEN ATTACK, THEY NEVERTHELESS SUCCEEDED IN DEVELOPING A WIDE RANGE OF INNOVATIVE TECHNIQUES....HORTICULTURE WAS THE MAINSTAY OF MOST MAROON ECONOMIES, WITH A SIMILAR LIST OF CULTIGENS APPEARING IN REPORTS FROM ALL AREAS -- MANIOC, YAMS, SWEET POTATOES, AND OTHER ROOT CROPS, BANANAS AND PLANTAINS, DRY RICE, MAIZE, GROUNDNUTS, SQUASH, BEANS, CHILE, SUGAR CANE, ASSORTED OTHER VEGETABLES, AND TOBACCO AND COTTON. THESE SEEM TO HAVE BEEN PLANTED IN A SIMILAR PATTERN OF INTERCROPPING -- FOR EXAMPLE, VEGETABLES SCATTERED IN A FIELD OF RICE -- FROM ONE END OF THE HEMISPHERE TO THE OTHER....WHENEVER NEW MAROONS ARRIVE, FOOD IS FURNISHED THEM BY THE OTHER MEMBERS, UNTIL THEY HAVE CLEARED A SPACE FOR A GARDEN AND THEIR CROPS ARE READY TO BE EATEN. WHENEVER LAND HAS TO BE CLEARED, EVERYONE WORKS TOGETHER, AND ONCE A LARGE AREA HAS BEEN BURNED, EVERYONE IS ALLOTTED A PLOT ACCORDING TO THE NEEDS OF THEIR FAMILY TO PLANT AND MAINTAIN."
(MAROON SOCIETIES, P10 AND 315)

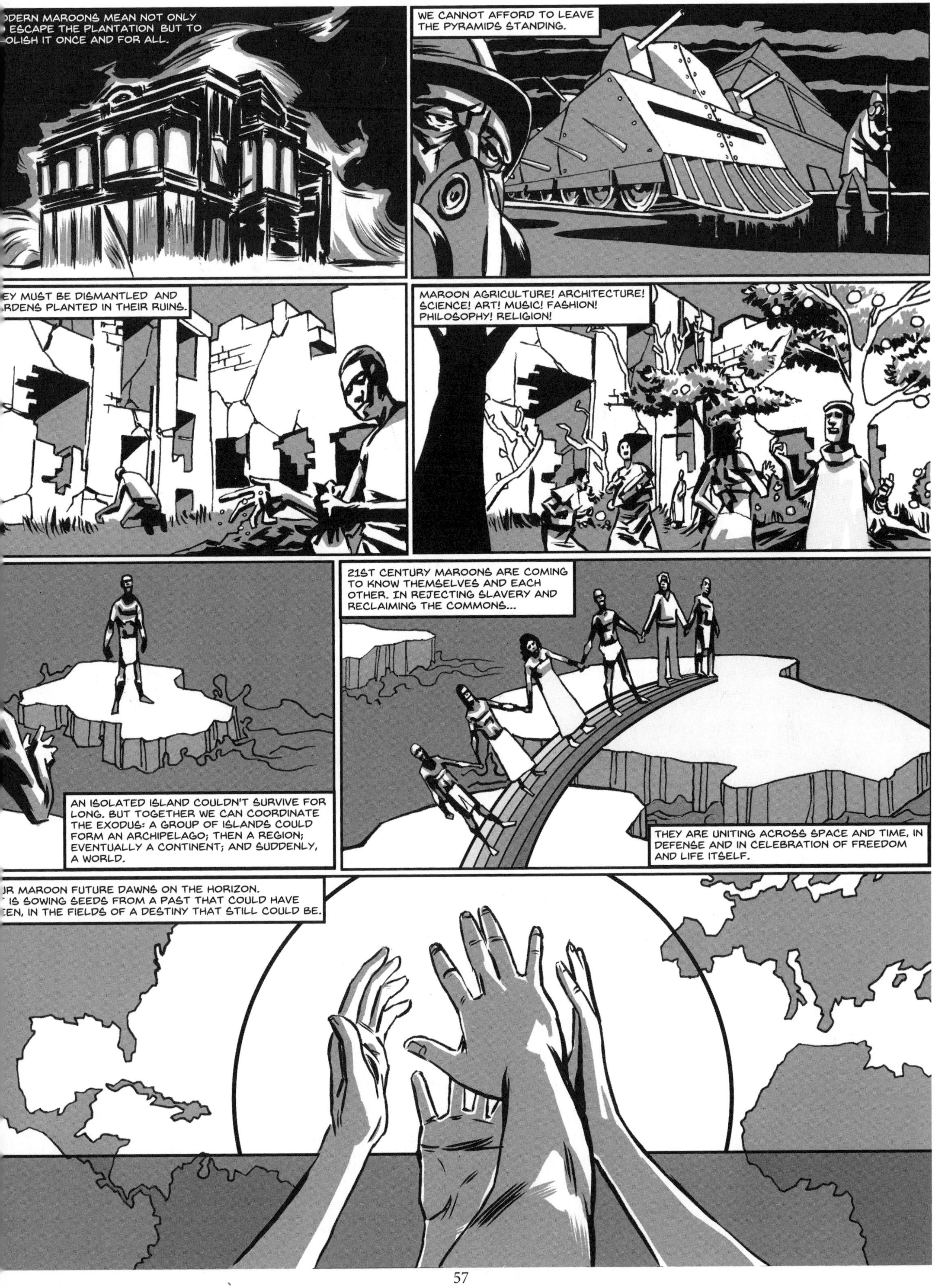
ODERN MAROONS MEAN NOT ONLY
ESCAPE THE PLANTATION BUT TO
OLISH IT ONCE AND FOR ALL.
WE CANNOT AFFORD TO LEAVE THE PYRAMIDS STANDING.
EY MUST BE DISMANTLED AND
ARDENS PLANTED IN THEIR RUINS.
MAROON AGRICULTURE! ARCHITECTURE! SCIENCE! ART! MUSIC! FASHION! PHILOSOPHY! RELIGION!
AN ISOLATED ISLAND COULDN'T SURVIVE FOR LONG. BUT TOGETHER WE CAN COORDINATE THE EXODUS: A GROUP OF ISLANDS COULD FORM AN ARCHIPELAGO; THEN A REGION; EVENTUALLY A CONTINENT; AND SUDDENLY, A WORLD.
21ST CENTURY MAROONS ARE COMING TO KNOW THEMSELVES AND EACH OTHER. IN REJECTING SLAVERY AND RECLAIMING THE COMMONS...
THEY ARE UNITING ACROSS SPACE AND TIME, IN DEFENSE AND IN CELEBRATION OF FREEDOM AND LIFE ITSELF.
JR MAROON FUTURE DAWNS ON THE HORIZON.
IS SOWING SEEDS FROM A PAST THAT COULD HAVE
EEN, IN THE FIELDS OF A DESTINY THAT STILL COULD BE.

Maroon Comix
Origins and Destinies

(a vision quest/manifesto)

Quincy Saul

The first written words about maroons were in the languages and books of their enemies. So the memory of their truth and their beauty survived in spite of the printed page. But through the centuries of slavery and empire, colonialism and capitalism, plantations and penitentiaries, a primary source more powerful than paper has echoed; in myths and legends, whispers and war cries, songs and recipes, dances and rituals.

"The maroon's vocation," as Édouard Glissant defines it, is "to be permanently opposed to everything down below, the plain and the people enslaved to it, and thus to find the strength to survive."[1] They made miracles in the mountains, summoned new societies in the swamps, forged new freedoms in the forests. They didn't just escape and steal from plantations—they also planted and harvested polycultures. They not only fought slavery, but they proved its opposite, and for generations they defended it, with blood and brilliance.

Historians try to tell the true stories of maroons. They search the diaries and account books of their captors and assassins for clues about their lives. Yet maroon memory is alive because like the maroons it stayed hidden. And so to tell maroon history is a paradox: How to reveal the majesty with reverence for the mystery? How to tell their story in a form which fits their freedom?

> You say "History" but that means nothing. So many lives, so many destinies, so many tracks go into the making of our unique path. You dare say History, but I say histories, *stories*. The one you take for the master stem of our manioc is but one stem among many others.[2]

To honor this paradox presented by modern maroon Marie-Sophie Laborieux, we propose *Maroon Comix*. *Maroon Comix* are stories insurgent against singular History, armed with art. Not a chronology but a collage; a pattern and a program that reflects maroon realities. "In examining maroon societies we find ourselves everywhere confronted with 'mosaic' cultures"[3]—world-historic alliances and alloys of African, indigenous, and European cultures of resistance and resilience. Movements of Oppressed Sectors Acting In Concert.[4]

A mosaic and a manifesto, a genre and a genealogy, a maroon methodology! That's the dream of *Maroon Comix*—a fire on the mountain where maroon words and images meet to tell stories together. Stories of escape and homecoming, exile and belonging. Stories which converge on the summits of the human spirit, where the most dreadful degradation is overcome by the most daring dignity. Stories of the damned who consecrate their own salvation.

The purpose of *Maroon Comix* is not recitation but resurrection; "a prophetic vision of the past!"[5] To find ourselves in the past, and then in the present discover an alternative future. To conjure in our minds the memories of moments when everything was risked and everything was at stake; to convoke those places where freedom conquered horror, and to summon that ancestral inheritance into the here and now.

Maroon Comix seek to succeed where maroon histories have failed. "Books rarely give you the feeling that you might never come back," writes Andrei Codrescu, "which was always a possibility in the mountains."[6] This book is an invitation to never go back, to join hands and hearts across space and time with the maroons and the mountains which await their return.

We are all hostages to mass media. The image reigns supreme. "In another generation," Codrescu feared, "people raised by images will not be able to imagine escape."[7] But just like the first maroons raided plantations for tools and supplies, so we raid the Image and the Word. In the autonomous zone of *Maroon Comix*, where freedom from converges with freedom to, the Image may help the Word escape from the West, and the Word may help the Image escape from the Screen. A Vision Quest to escape the Society of the Spectacle! This is *Maroon Comix*: the kindling of a quilombo in our hearts and minds, and fresh water for the roots of an old garden, where freedom still blossoms, where wild words wander among implacable images.

But this book is not the whole story, not the master stem of the manioc. At best it's a beginning, not the last of its kind but the first. This is an invitation and initiation into the origins and destinies of maroons. If you've come this far, then the next episodes are up to you.

Notes

1. *The Fourth Century*, by Édouard Glissant, p141
2. Marie-Sophie Laborieux quoted in *Texaco*, by Patrick Chamoiseau, p88
3. Roger Bastide quoted in *Maroon Societies*, edited by Richard Price, p26
4. *Maroon the Implacable*, by Russell Maroon Shoatz, p127
5. *Caribbean Discourse*, by Édouard Glissant, p64
6. *A Manifesto for Escape*, by Andrei Codrescu, p12
7. Ibid., p113

Maroon Library

compiled by Quincy Saul

(with thanks to Matt Meyer and Richard Price)

Cited in Maroon Comix

American Negro Slave Revolts, by Herbert Aptheker. International Publishers, 1983.

"breathing manifesto: a new black arts movement," at https://anewblackartsmovement.com/about/.

Fukushima Mon Amour, by Sabu Kohso et al. Autonomedia, 2011.

Gone to Croatan: Origins of North American Dropout Culture, edited by Ron Sakolsky and James Koehnline. Autonomedia, 1994.

A History of Pan-African Revolt, by C.L.R. James. PM Press, 2012.

Jailbreak Out of History: The Re-Biography of Harriet Tubman, by Butch Lee. Kersplebedeb, 2000.

Liberating Life: Woman's Revolution, by Abdullah Öcalan. International Initiative, 2011.

The Maroons of Jamaica 1655–1796: A History of Resistance, Collaboration and Betrayal, by Mavis Campbell. Africa World Press, 1990.

Maroon Societies: Rebel Slave Communities in the Americas, by Richard Price. Johns Hopkins University Press, 1979.

Maroon the Implacable: The Collected Writings of Russell Maroon Shoatz, edited by Fred Ho and Quincy Saul. PM Press, 2013.

The Serpent and the Rainbow: A Harvard Scientist's Astonishing Journey into the Secret Societies of Haitian Voodoo, Zombies, and Magic, by Wade Davis. Simon and Schuster, 1985.

"The Sixth Declaration of the Selva Lacandona." Zapatista Army of National Liberation. Enlace Zapatista, June 2005, at http://enlacezapatista.ezln.org.mx/sdsl-en/.

"Statement by Gaanman Joachim-Joseph Adochini, Paramount Chief of the Aluku (Boni) People," translated by Kenneth Bilby, Smithsonian Folklife Festival, 1992, at https://folklife.si.edu/resources/maroon/educational_guide/57.htm.

Texaco, by Patrick Chamoiseau, Vintage, 1998.

Ujamaa: Essays on Socialism, by Julius Nyerere. Oxford University Press, 1974.

The Village against the World, by Dan Hancox. Verso, 2014.

Maroon History and the Revolt of the Enslaved

Agorsah, E. Kofi, ed. *Maroon Heritage: Archaeological, Ethnographic, and Historical Perspectives*. Canoe Press, 1994.

Aptheker, Herbert. *To Be Free: Studies in American Negro History*. International Publishers, 1968.

Aptheker, Herbert. *American Negro Slave Revolts*. International Publishers, 1983.

Barnet, Miguel, and Esteban Montejo. *Biography of a Runaway Slave*. Curbstone Press, 1994.

Bastide, Roger, *The African Religions of Brazil: Toward a Sociology of the Interpenetration of Civilizations*. Translated by Helen Sebba. Johns Hopkins University Press, 2007.

Bilby, Kenneth M. *True-Born Maroons*. University Press of Florida, 2005.

Bontemps, Arna. *Black Thunder: Gabriel's Revolt: Virginia, 1800*. Beacon Press, 1992.

Campbell, Mavis. *The Maroons of Jamaica 1655–1796: A History of Resistance, Collaboration and Betrayal*. Africa World Press, 1990.

Cheney, Glenn Alan. *Quilombo dos Palmares: Brazil's Lost Nation of Fugitive Slaves*. New London Librarium, 2014.

Cooper, Melissa L. *Making Gullah: A History of Sapelo Islanders, Race, and the American Imagination*. University of North Carolina Press, 2017.

Dallas, Robert Charles. *The History of the Maroons: From Their Origin to the Establishment of Their Chief Tribe at Sierra Leone*. Amazon Digital Services, 2013.

Davis, Wade. *The Serpent and the Rainbow: A Harvard Scientist's Astonishing Journey into the Secret Societies of Haitian Voodoo, Zombies, and Magic*. Simon and Schuster, 1985.

Diouf, Sylviane A. *Slavery's Exiles: The Story of the American Maroons*. NYU Press, 2014.

Douglass, Frederick. *Narrative of the Life of Frederick Douglass, An American Slave: Written by Himself*. Anchor Books, 1989.

Federici, Silvia. *Caliban and the Witch: Women, the Body and Primitive Accumulation*. Autonomedia, 2004.

Foner, Eric. *Gateway to Freedom: The Hidden History of the Underground Railroad*. W.W. Norton and Company, 2015.

Fouchard, Jean. *The Haitian Maroons: Liberty or Death*. Edward Blyden, 1981.

Franklin, John Hope, and Loren Schweninger. *Runaway Slaves: Rebels on the Plantation*. Oxford University Press, 2000.

Galeano, Eduardo. *The Memory of Fire Trilogy: Genesis, Faces and Masks, and Century of the Wind*. Nation Books, 2010.

Galeano, Eduardo. *Mirrors: Stories of Almost Everyone*. Nation Books, 2010.

Garvey, Marcus. *Philosophy and Opinions of Marcus Garvey*. Edited by Amy Jacques-Garvey. Martino Fine Books, 2014.

Genovese, Eugene D. *From Rebellion to Revolution: Afro-American Slave Revolts in the Making of the Modern World*. LSU Press, 1992.

Giddings, Joshua R. *The Exiles of Florida*. Black Classic Press, 1997.

Gottlieb, Karla. *The Mother of Us All: A History of Queen Nanny, Leader of the Windward Jamaican Maroons*. Africa World Press, 2000.

Herne, Gerald. *The Counter-Revolution of 1776: Slave Resistance and the Origins of the United States of America*. NYU Press, 2016.

Herskovits, Melville Jean, and Frances S. Herskovits. *Rebel Destiny: Among the Bush Negroes of Dutch Guiana*. McGraw-Hill, 1934.

Heuman, Gad, ed. *Out of the House of Bondage: Runaways, Resistance and Marronage in Africa and the New World*. Routledge, 1986.

Ho, Fred, and Quincy Saul, ed. *Maroon the Implacable: The Collected Writings of Russell Maroon Shoatz*. PM Press, 2013.

Hoogbergen, Wim S.M. *The Boni Maroon Wars in Suriname*. Brill, 1997.

James, C.L.R. *The Black Jacobins*. Random House, 1963.

James, C.L.R. *A History of Pan-African Revolt*. PM Press, 2012.

Katz, William Loren. *Black Indians: A Hidden Heritage*. Athenaeum, 1997.

La Rosa Corzo, Gabino. *Runaway Slave Settlements in Cuba: Resistance and Repression*. Translated by Mary Todd. University of North Carolina Press, 2003.

Landers, Jane, and Barry Robinson, ed. *Slaves, Subjects, and Subversives: Blacks in Colonial America*. University of New Mexico Press, 2006.

Leaming, Hugo Prosper. *Hidden Americans: Maroons of Virginia and the Carolinas*. Garland, 1995.

Lee, Butch. *Jailbreak Out of History: The Re-Biography of Harriet Tubman*. Kersplebedeb, 2000, at http://kersplebedeb.com/posts/jailbreak/.

Linebaugh, Peter, and Marcus Rediker. *The Many-Headed Hydra: Sailors, Slaves, Commoners, and the Hidden History of the Revolutionary Atlantic*. Beacon Press, 2000.

Lockley, Timothy James, ed. *Maroon Communities in South Carolina: A Documentary Record*. University of South Carolina Press, 2009.

Lynch, Hollis R. *Edward Wilmot Blyden: Pan-Negro Patriot*. Oxford University Press, 1970.

McFarlane, Milton C. *Cudjoe the Maroon*. Allison and Busby, 1977.

Montejo, Esteban. *The Autobiography of a Runaway Slave*. Pantheon, 1968.

Mulroy, Kevin. *Freedom on the Border: The Seminole Maroons in Florida, the Indian Territory, Coahuila, and Texas*. Texas Tech University Press, 2003.

Patterson, Orlando. *Slavery and Social Death: A Comparative Study*. Harvard University Press, 1985.

Pattullo, Polly, ed. *Your Time Is Done Now: Slavery, Resistance, and Defeat: The Maroon Trials of Dominica (1813–1814)*. Monthly Review Press, 2016.

Price, Richard. *The Guiana Maroons: A Historical and Bibliographical Introduction*. Johns Hopkins University Press, 1976.

Price, Richard. *Maroon Societies: Rebel Slave Communities in the Americas*. Johns Hopkins University Press, 1979.

Price, Richard. *First-Time: The Historical Vision of an Afro-American People*. Johns Hopkins University Press, 1983.

Price, Richard. *Alabi's World*. Johns Hopkins University Press, 1990.

Price, Richard, and Sally Price. *Two Evenings in Saramaka*. University of Chicago Press, 1991.

Price, Richard, and Sally Price. *Saamaka Dreaming*. Duke University Press, 2017.

Price, Sally. *Co-Wives and Calabashes*. University of Michigan Press, 1984.

Reis, José, and Flávio dos Santos Gomes, ed. *Freedom by a Thread: The History of Quilombos in Brazil*. Diasporic Africa Press, 2016.

Robinson, Carey. *The Fighting Maroons of Jamaica*. William Collins and Sangster, 1971.

Still, William. *Underground Railroad*. Dover, 2007.

Styron, William. *The Confessions of Nat Turner*. Vintage, 1992.

Thoden van Velzen, H.U.E., and W. Van Wetering. *In the Shadow of the Oracle: Religion as Politics in a Suriname Maroon Society*. Waveland Press, 2004.

Thomas, Lamont D. *Paul Cuffe: Black Entrepreneur and Pan-Africanist*. University of Illinois Press, 1988.

Thompson, Alvin O. *Flight to Freedom: African Runaways and Maroons in the Americas*. University of the West Indies Press, 2006.

Walzer, Michael. *Exodus and Revolution*. Basic Books, 1985.

Williams, Eric. *Capitalism and Slavery*. University of North Carolina Press, 1994.

Zips, Werner. *Nanny's Asafo Warriors: The Jamaican Maroons' African Experience*. Ian Randle, 2012.

Maroon Philosophy

Amin, Samir. *Delinking: Towards a Polycentric World*. Zed Books, 1990.

Ciccariello-Maher, George. *Decolonizing Dialectics*. Duke University Press, 2017.

Clark, John P. *The Impossible Community: Realizing Communitarian Anarchism*. Bloomsbury, 2013.

Deleuze, Gilles, and Félix Guattari. *Nomadology: The War Machine*. Semiotext(e), 1986.

Dussel, Enrique. *The Underside of Modernity: Apel, Ricoeur, Rorty, Taylor, and the Philosophy of Liberation*. Humanities Press, 1996.

Glaberman, Martin, ed. *Marxism for Our Times: C.L.R. James on Revolutionary Organization*. University Press of Mississippi, 1999.

Glissant, Édouard. *Caribbean Discourse: Selected Essays*. University Press of Virginia, 1989.

Harney, Stefano, and Fred Moten. *The Undercommons: Fugitive Planning and Black Study*. Autonomedia, 2013.

Holloway, John. *Change the World Without Taking Power: The Meaning of Revolution Today*. Pluto Press, 2005.

Jackson, George L. *Blood in My Eye*. Black Classic Press, 1996.

Kelley, Robin D.G. *Freedom Dreams: The Black Radical Imagination*. Beacon, 2002.

Mies, Maria, and Veronika Bennholdt-Thomsen. *The Subsistence Perspective: Beyond the Globalized Economy*. Zed Books, 1999.

Nyerere, Julius K. *Ujamaa: Essays on Socialism*. Oxford University Press, 1974.

Öcalan, Abdullah. *Manifesto for a Democratic Civilization, Volume 1: The Age of Masked Gods and Disguised Kings*. New Compass Press, 2015.

Roberts, Neil. *Freedom as Marronage*. University of Chicago Press, 2015.

Saucier, P. Khalil, and Tryon P. Woods, ed. *On Marronage: Ethical Confrontations with Antiblackness*. Africa World Press, 2015.

Smith, Linda Tuhiwai. *Decolonizing Methodologies: Research and Indigenous Peoples*. Zed Books, 2012.

Wolin, Sheldon S. *Fugitive Democracy and Other Essays*. Princeton University Press, 2016.

Whiteness and Maroons of European Descent

Allen, Theodore W. *The Invention of the White Race.* Verso, 2012.

Breytenbach, Breyten. *The True Confessions of an Albino Terrorist.* McGraw-Hill, 1986.

Brodkin, Karen. *How Jews Became White Folks and What that Says about Race in America.* Rutgers University Press, 1998.

Buhle, Paul. *Robin Hood: People's Outlaw and Forest Hero.* PM Press, 2011.

Cabeza de Vaca, Álvar Núñez. *The Narrative of Cabeza de Vaca.* University of Nebraska Press, 2003 [1905].

Du Bois, W.E.B. *John Brown.* International Publishers, 1962.

Gilbert, David. *No Surrender: Writings from an Anti-imperialist Political Prisoner.* Abraham Guillen Press / Arm the Spirit, 2004.

Gilbert, David. *Love and Struggle: My Life in SDS, the Weather Underground, and Beyond.* PM Press, 2011.

Ignatiev, Noel. *How the Irish Became White.* Routledge, 1995.

Ignatiev, Noel, and John Garvey, ed. *Race Traitor.* Routledge, 1996.

Kovel, Joel. *White Racism: A Psychohistory.* Columbia University Press, 1994.

Kovel, Joel. *The Lost Traveller's Dream: A Memoir.* Autonomedia, 2017.

Lawrence, T.E. *Seven Pillars of Wisdom.* Anchor, 1991 [1922].

Linebaugh, Peter. *The Magna Carta Manifesto: Liberties and Commons for All.* University of California Press, 2009.

Morton, Thomas. *New English Canaan.* Edited by Jack Dempsey. Jack Dempsey, 2000.

Oates, Stephen B. *To Purge this Land with Blood: A Biography of John Brown.* University of Massachusetts Press, 1984.

Painter, Nell Irvin. *The History of White People.* W.W. Norton and Company, 2011.

Rediker, Marcus. *Villains of All Nations: Atlantic Pirates in the Golden Age.* Beacon Press, 2004.

Rodgers, Nini. *Ireland: Slavery and Anti-Slavery: 1612–1867.* Palgrave Macmillan, 2007.

Sachs, Albie. *Soft Vengeance of a Freedom Fighter.* University of California Press, 2014.

Sakai, J. *Settlers: The Myth of the White Proletariat from Mayflower to Modern.* PM Press, 2015.

Sakolsky, Ron, and James Koehnline, ed. *Gone to Croatan: Origins of North American Dropout Culture.* Autonomedia, 1994.

Segrest, Mab. *Memoir of a Race Traitor.* South End Press, 1999.

Wilson, Peter Lamborn. *Pirate Utopias: Moorish Corsairs and European Renegadoes.* Autonomedia, 2003.

Marooning in the Twentieth and Twenty-First Centuries

Africa Information Service, ed. *Unity and Struggle: Speeches and Writings of Amilcar Cabral.* Monthly Review Press, 1979.

Akuno, Kali, and Ajamu Nangwaya, ed. *Jackson Rising: The Struggle for Economic Democracy and Self-Determination in Jackson, Mississippi.* Daraja Press, 2017.

Balagoon, Kuwasi. *A Soldier's Story: Writings by a Revolutionary New Afrikan Anarchist.* Kersplebedeb, 2003.

Banks, Dennis, with Richard Erdoes. *Ojibwa Warrior: Dennis Banks and the Rise of the American Indian Movement.* University of Oklahoma Press, 2005.

Bey, Hakim. *T.A.Z.: The Temporary Autonomous Zone, Ontological Anarchy, Poetic Terrorism.* Autonomedia, 2003.

Bin Wahad, Dhoruba, Assata Shakur, and Mumia Abu-Jamal. *Still Black, Still Strong: Survivors of the War Against Black Revolutionaries.* Semiotext(e), 1993.

Boggs, Grace Lee, with Scott Kurashige. *The Next American Revolution: Sustainable Activism for the Twenty-First Century.* University of California Press, 2012.

Bukhari, Safiya. *The War Before: The True Life Story of Becoming a Black Panther, Keeping the Faith in Prison, and Fighting for Those Left Behind.*, Feminist Press at CUNY, 2010.

Codrescu, Andrei. *The Disappearance of the Outside: A Manifesto for Escape.* Addison-Wesley, 1990.

Cohen, Robert Carl. *Black Crusader: A Biography of Robert Franklin Williams.* Jorvik Press, 2015.

Corretjer, Juan Antonio. *Albizu Campos and the Ponce Massacre.* New York: World View Publishers, 1965.

CR10 Publications Collective. *Abolition Now! Ten Years of Strategy and Struggle Against the Prison Industrial Complex.* AK Press, 2008.

Davis, Angela Y. *Freedom Is a Constant Struggle: Ferguson, Palestine, and the Foundations of a Movement.* Haymarket Books, 2016.

de Roulet, Daniel, Anne Waldman, Silvia Federici, George Caffentzis, and Sabu Kohso. *Fukushima Mon Amour.* Autonomedia, 2011.

Dirik, Dilar, David Levi Strauss, Michael Taussig, and Peter Lamborn Wilson, ed. *To Dare Imagining: Rojava Revolution.* Autonomedia, 2016.

El Kilombo Intergalactico. *Beyond Resistance: Everything: An Interview with Subcomandante Insurgente Marcos.* PaperBoat Press, 2007.

Goff, Stan. *Sex and War.* Soft Skull Press, 2006.

Gutiérrez Aguilar, Raquel. *Rhythms of the Pachakuti: Indigenous Uprising and State Power in Bolivia.* Duke University Press, 2014.

Hancox, Dan. *The Village Against the World.* Verso, 2014.

Hilliard, Asa G. *The Maroon Within Us: Selected Essays on African American Community Socialization.* Black Classic Press, 1995.

Ibbott, Ralph. *Ujamaa: The Hidden History of Tanzania's Socialist Villages.* Edited by Nina Lopez and Selma James. Crossroads Books, 2014.

James, Joy, ed. *The New Abolitionists: (Neo)slave Narratives and Contemporary Prison Writings.* State University of New York Press, 2005.

Johnson, Kevin "Rashid." *Defying the Tomb: Selected Prison Writings and Art of Kevin "Rashid" Johnson, Featuring Exchanges with an Outlaw.* Kersplebedeb, 2010.

Khoisan, Zenzile. *Jakaranda Time: An Investigator's View of South Africa's Truth and Reconciliation Commission.* Garib Press, 2001.

kioni-sadiki, déqui, and Matt Meyer, ed. *Look for Me in the Whirlwind: From the Panther 21 to 21st Century Revolutions.* With new commentary by Sekou Odinga, Dhoruba Bin Wahad, Shaba Om, and Jamal Joseph. PM Press, 2017.

López Rivera, Oscar. *Between Torture and Resistance.* Edited by Luis Nieves Falcón. PM Press, 2013.

Melucci, Alberto. *Nomads of the Present: Social Movements and Individual Needs in Contemporary Society.* Temple University Press, 1989.

Meyer, Matt, ed. *Let Freedom Ring: A Collection of Documents from the Movements to Free U.S. Political Prisoners.* PM Press, 2008.

Miller, Ron, and Rob Williams, ed. *Most Likely to Secede: What the Vermont Independence Movement Can Teach Us about Reclaiming Community and Creating a Human Scale Vision for the 21st Century.* Vermont Independence Press, 2013.

Moore, Alan W. *Occupation Culture: Art and Squatting in the City from Below*. Minor Compositions, 2015.

Muntaqim, Jalil A. *We Are Our Own Liberators*. Abraham Guillen Press, 2000.

Negri, Antonio, and Michael Hardt. *Commonwealth*. Harvard University Press, 2009.

Obadele, Imari Abubakari. *War in America: The Malcolm X Doctrine*. Malcolm X Society, 1968.

Öcalan, Abdullah. *War and Peace in Kurdistan*. International Initiative 2009.

Öcalan, Abdullah. *Liberating Life: Woman's Revolution*. International Initiative, 2011.

Price, Richard. *Rainforest Warriors: Human Rights on Trial*. University of Pennsylvania Press, 2012.

Price, Sally, and Richard Price. *Maroon Arts: Cultural Vitality in the African Diaspora*. Beacon Press, 1999.

Rameau, Max. *Take Back the Land: Land, Gentrification and the Umoja Village Shantytown*. Nia Press, 2008.

Saul, Quincy, Fred Ho, and Seth Tobocman. *Truth and Dare: A Comic Book Curriculum for the End and the Beginning of the World*. Ecosocialist Horizons and Autonomedia, 2014.

Shakur, Assata. *Assata: An Autobiography*. Lawrence Hill Books, 2001.

Shakur, Sanyika. *Monster: The Autobiography of an L.A. Gang Member*. Grove Press, 1993.

Smith, Paul Chaat, and Robert Allen Warrior. *Like a Hurricane: The Indian Movement from Alcatraz to Wounded Knee*. The New Press, 1997.

Squatting Europe Kollective, ed. *The Squatters' Movement in Europe: Commons and Autonomy as Alternatives to Capitalism*. Pluto Press, 2014.

Subcomandante Insurgente Marcos. *Our Word Is Our Weapon*. Seven Stories Press, 2002.

Turner, Terisa A., with Bryan J. Ferguson, ed. *Arise Ye Mighty People! Gender, Class and Race in Popular Struggles*. Africa World Press, 1994.

Van Deburg, William L. *New Day in Babylon: The Black Power Movement and American Culture, 1965–1975*. University of Chicago Press, 1993.

Van der Steen, Bart, Ask Katzeff, and Leendert van Hoogenhuijze, ed. *The City Is Ours: Squatting and Autonomous Movements in Europe from the 1970s to Present*. PM Press, 2014.

Voeten, Teun. *Tunnel People*. PM Press, 2010.

Waterman Wittstock, Laura, and Dick Bancroft. *We Are Still Here: A Photographic History of the American Indian Movement*. Borealis Books, 2013.

Weisman, Alan. *Gaviotas: A Village to Reinvent the World*. Chelsea Green Publishing, 2008.

Zapatista Army of National Liberation. *Shadows of Tender Fury: The Letters and Communiqués of Subcomandante Marcos and the Zapatista Army of National Liberation*. Monthly Review, 1995.

Zibechi, Raúl. *Dispersing Power: Social Movements as Anti-State Forces*. AK Press, 2010.

Zibechi, Raúl. *Territories in Resistance: A Cartography of Latin American Social Movements*. AK Press, 2012.

Maroons in the East

Ariyaratne, Vinya. "The 500 Year Peace Plan." 2000, at http://www.commonway.org/sarvodaya-peace-action-plan.

Figes, Orlando. *Peasant Russia, Civil War: The Volga Countryside in Revolution 1917–1921*. Clarendon Press, 1989.

Fukuoka, Masanobu. *The One Straw Revolution: An Introduction to Natural Farming*. New York Review, 2009.

Gandhi, M.K. *Village Swaraj*. Navajivan Trust, 2014.

Katsiaficas, George. *Asia's Unknown Uprisings Volume 1: South Korean Social Movements in the 20th Century*, PM Press, 2012.

Katsiaficas, George. *Asia's Unknown Uprisings Volume 2: People Power in the Philippines, Burma, Tibet, China, Taiwan, Bangladesh, Nepal, Thailand, and Indonesia*. PM Press, 2013.

Liyanage, Gunadasa. *Revolution under the Breadfruit Tree: The Story of the Sarvodaya Shramadana Movement and Its Founder Dr. A.T. Ariyaratne*. Sinha Publishers, 1988.

Narayan, Jayaprakash. *Socialism, Sarvodaya and Democracy*. Edited by Bimla Prasad. Asia Publishing House, 1964.

Narayan, Jayaprakash. *Towards Total Revolution: India and Her Problems*. Richmond Publishing Company, 1979.

Ramnath, Maia. *Decolonizing Anarchism*. AK Press, 2012.

Scott, James C. *The Art of Not Being Governed: An Anarchist History of Upland Southeast Asia*. Yale University Press, 2009.

Shanin, Teodor. *Late Marx and the Russian Road: Marx and "The Peripheries of Capitalism."* Monthly Review, 1983.

Stetler, Russell, ed. *The Military Art of People's War: Selected Writings of General by Vo Nguyen Giap*. Monthly Review Press, 1970.

Maroon Literature

Amaworo Wilson, JJ. *Damnificados*. PM Press, 2016.

Bisson, Terry. *Fire on the Mountain*. PM Press, 2009.

Breytenbach, Breytan. *Mouroir*. Archipelago, 2009.

Carpentier, Alejo. *The Kingdom of This World*. Farrar, Straus and Giroux, 2006 [1949].

Chamoiseau, Patrick. *Texaco*. Vintage, 1998.

Cliff, Michelle. *Abeng*. Plume, 1995.

Cliff, Michelle. *No Telephone to Heaven*. Plume, 1996.

Condé, Maryse. *Crossing the Mangrove*. Anchor, 1995.

Delany, Martin R. *Blake, or The Huts of America*. Beacon Press, 1971.

Douglass, Frederick. *The Heroic Slave*. John P. Jewett and Company, 1852.

D'Salete, Marcelo. *Run for It: Stories of Slaves Who Fought for Their Freedom*. Fantagraphics Books, 2017.

Endore, Guy. *Babouk*. Monthly Review Press, 1991.

Glissant, Édouard. *The Fourth Century*. Bison Books, 2001.

Ho Chí Minh. *Prison Poems and Selected Writings*. University Press of the Pacific, 2001.

Huxley, Aldous. *Island*. Harper, 2009.

James, Marlon. *The Book of Night Women*. Riverhead Books, 2010.

Le Guin, Ursula K. *Always Coming Home*. Bantam Books, 1985.

Le Guin, Ursula K. *The Dispossessed*. Harper Voyager, 1994.

Marcus, Martin L. *Freedom Land*. Forge Books, 2003.

Robson, Lucia St. Clair. *Light a Distant Fire*. Ballantine Books, 1991.

Schwarz-Bart. André. *A Woman Named Solitude*. Atheneum, 1973.

Turso, Betty. *John Horse: Florida's First Freedom Fighter*. CreateSpace Independent Publishing Platform, 2014.

Unsworth, Barry. *Sacred Hunger*. W.W. Norton and Company, 1993.

Wideman, John Edgar. *Philadelphia Fire*. Mariner Books, 2005.

Wright, Richard. *Black Power: Three Books from Exile*. Harper, 2008.

Maroon Movies

Anderson, Roy T., dir. *Queen Nanny: Legendary Maroon Chieftainess*. 2016.

Brownlow, Kevin, and Andrew Mollo, dir. *Winstanley*. 1975.

Coney, John, dir. *Space Is the Place*. Written by Joshua Smith and Sun Ra. 1974.

Dash, Julie, dir. *Daughters of the Dust*. 1991.

Diegues, Carlos, dir. *Ganga Zumba*. 1963.

Diegues, Carlos, dir. *Quilombo*. 1985.

Gerima, Haile, dir. *Sankofa*. 1996.

Hershfield, Joanne, dir. *Mama C: Urban Warrior in the African Bush*. 2014.

Jarmusch, Jim, dir. *Dead Man*. 1996.

Noyce, Philip, dir. *Rabbit-Proof Fence*. Based on the book *Follow the Rabbit-Proof Fence* by Doris Pilkington. 2002.

Olsson, Göran, dir, *The Black Power Mixtape 1965–1975*. 2011.

Olsson, Göran, dir. *Concerning Violence*. 2014.

Osder, Jason, dir. *Let the Fire Burn*. 2014.

Pontecorvo, Gillo, dir. *Burn!*. 1969.

Pontecorvo, Gillo, dir. *The Battle of Algiers*. 2004 [1966].

Rolando, Gloria, dir. *The Eyes of the Rainbow*. A film about Assata Shakur. 1997.

Van Peebles, Melvin, dir. *Sweet Sweetback's Baadasssss Song*. 1971.

Maroon Articles

Bilby, Kenneth, and Diana Baird N'Diaye. "Creativity and Resistance: Maroon Cultures." *Festival of American Folklife Catalog*, 1992.

Bilby, Kenneth, trans. "Statement by Gaanman Joachim-Joseph Adochini, Paramount Chief of the Aluku (Boni) People." Smithsonian Folklife Festival, 1992, at https://folklife.si.edu/resources/maroon/educational_guide/57.htm

"breathing manifesto: a new black arts movement," at https://anewblackartsmovement.com/about/.

Grant, Richard. "Deep in the Swamp, Archaeologists are Finding How Fugitive Slaves Kept Their Freedom." *Smithsonian Magazine*, September 2016.

"Historical Meeting Between the Kingdom of Ashanti and the Accompong Maroons in Jamaica." *Modern Ghana, Diaspora News*, May 2, 2016.

Ho, Fred. "Revolutionary Maroons: Coming to a Class Struggle Theater Near You . . ." *New Clear Vision*, June 2013.

Ho, Fred, with Matt Meyer. "Toward a Maroon Society: Working Together to Build a New World." *New Clear Vision*, June 2013.

Lause, Mark A. "Borderland Visions: Maroons and Outliers in Early American History." *Monthly Review*, September 2002.

Nyerere, Julius. "The Arusha Declaration," February 5, 1967, at https://www.marxists.org/subject/africa/nyerere/1967/arusha-declaration.htm.

Price, Richard. "Refiguring Palmares." *Tipiti: Journal of the Society for the Anthropology of Lowland Latin America*, December 2003.

Price, Richard. "Saamaka Gays in Quilombos?" *Revista de Historia Comparada*, vol. 7, no. 1, 2013.

Price, Richard. "The Maroon Population Explosion: Suriname and Guyane." *New West Indian Guide*, vol. 87, no. 3–4, 2013.

Sudbury, Julia. "Maroon Abolitionists: Black Gender-oppressed Activists in the Anti-Prison Movement in the U.S. and Canada." *Meridians*, vol. 1, no. 9, 2009.

Zapatista Army of National Liberation. "The Sixth Declaration of the Selva Lacondona." *Enlace Zapatista*, June 2005, at http://enlacezapatista.ezln.org.mx/sdsl-en/.

Maroon Music

The C.I.P.H.E.R. Chapter 1: The Pioneers. Commusaic, 2016.

Drums of Defiance: Maroon Music from the Earliest Free Black Communities of Jamaica. Smithsonian Folkways, 1992.

From Slavery to Freedom: Music of the Saramaka Maroons of Suriname. Produced and recorded by Verna Gillis. Annotated by Richard Price. Lyrichord, 1981.

Maroon Music. By Adetokunbo. 2015, at www.hatedsaints.com.

Maroon Law. By Adetokunbo. 2016, at www.hatedsaints.com.

Maroons: Ambush. By Lateef and the Chief. Quannum Projects, Epitaph Records, 2004.

Music from Aluku: Maroon Sounds of Struggle, Solace, and Survival. Recorded, compiled, and annotated by Kenneth Bilby. Smithsonian Folkways, 2011.

Music from Saramaka: A Dynamic Afro-American Tradition. Produced by Richard Price and Sally Price. Smithsonian Folkways, 1977.

The Music of Cal Massey: A Tribute. Produced by Fred Ho and Quincy Saul. Big Red Media, 2011.

Original Aloukou Soldiers. By Wailing Roots. Déclic Communication, 1994.

Ultimate Universe: Live at Lush Life Café Volume 4. By Bilal Sunni Ali. Path of Light Records, 2008.

Winter in America. By Gil Scott-Heron and Brian Jackson. Charly, 2010 [Strata-East, 1974].

Maroon Recipes

"Maroon Foodways." A collection of recipes from maroons in Jamaica, Suriname, Texas, Oklahoma, Mexico, Colombia, and French Guiana. Coordinated by James Deutsch, Kenneth Bilby, Diana N'Diaye, and Phyllis Agnelli-Lesansky, at http://www.folklife.si.edu/resources/maroon/foodways/marfood.htm.

About the Editor and Illustrators

Quincy Saul is a writer, musician, and co-founder of Ecosocialist Horizons. He is the co-editor of *Maroon the Implacable: The Collected Writings of Russell Maroon Shoatz*, the author of *Truth and Dare: A Comic Book Curriculum for the End and the Beginning of the World*, and the co-producer of *The Music of Cal Massey*.

Seth Tobocman is a comic book artist whose work often deals with political issues from a radical and independent point of view. He founded the magazine *World War 3 Illustrated* with Peter Kuper in 1979 and has been part of the editorial collective ever since. His work has appeared in the *New York Times*, the *Village Voice*, *Heavy Metal*, and many other magazines. He is author of a number of graphic books including: *You Don't Have to Fuck People Over to Survive*, *War in the Neighborhood*, *Portraits of Israelis and Palestinians*, *Disaster and Resistance*, *Understanding the Crash*, and *Len, A Lawyer in History*. Tobocman's art has been shown at the Museum of Modern Art, the New Museum of Contemporary Art, the Museum of the City of Ravenna, Exit Art, and ABC No Rio. His images have been used as posters, murals, banners, and tattoos by people's movements from squatters in New York's Lower East Side to the African National Congress in South Africa.

Mikaela González, recent graduate of Hampshire College, has dedicated her art, studies, and activism in western Massachusetts, Mexico, and Cuba to artistically spreading awareness, building community, celebrating identity, and creating space for radical collaboration. She sees her art as her tool for approaching liberation.

Songe Riddle was born in Los Angeles, California, in 1975. In adolescence he got involved in the American Punk scene and adjacent activist movements, and while a part of the New York squatter community enrolled at Parson's School of Design, where he studied illustration and animation. Songe has provided illustrations for too many people to name and likes to spend his time off doing much of the same of what he does when he's working.

Hannah Allen (H.E.N.A.) is a lifelong cartoonist who first met Quincy Saul when they had the privilege of working together in Hampshire College's Students for Justice in Palestine (dubbed the Order of the Phoenix by Allen), where they both helped lead a successful BDS campaign in the spring of 2009. H.E.N.A. earned a bachelor's degree from Hampshire College in 2010 in history with a focus on comparative revolutions. Before college, their childhood as a closeted queer and mentally ill artist led them to seek out stories and theories of resistance on a larger scale to better understand systems of oppression, and how to tear them down. In their free time, Allen is usually making art, politicizing conversations about fantasy and science fiction, and seeking out the next queer dance party.

Emmy Kepler is a nihilist wingnut and wiener dog lover based in Chicago.

Mac McGill's illustrations have appeared in magazines, newspapers, and books such as *The Progressive*, *Tikkun*, *The Source*, Mumia Abu-Jamal's *All Things Censored* (Seven Stories Press), *The Quotable Rebel: Political Quotations for Dangerous Time*s (Common Courage Press), *World War 3 Illustrated*, the *Amsterdam News*, *Squatter Comics*, the *City Sun*, the *Shadow*, *Voices of Resistance from Occupied London*, *Chimurenga Magazine* (South Africa), *Madburger* and *Warburger* (Slovenia), the *Black Panther Community News Service*, *High Times*, *Wobblies! A Graphic History of the Industrial Workers of the World* (Verso), the *Guardian Radical Newsweekly*, and *African-American Graphic Classics* (Eureka Productions). His work has been exhibited in New York City at ABC NO RIO, School of Visual Arts, Theater for the New City, Issue Project Room, Umbrella Haus, and the Cathedral of St. John the Divine ("The Value of Water"); as well as at Amadora BD in Portugal; the Babel Festival in Athens, Greece; the HU10 Underground Festival in Milan, Italy; the Forte Presentino in Rome; BlackWaxx in Jersey City, New Jersey; and the Library of Congress in Washington D.C. ("Timely and Timeless"). He is a native New Yorker living in the East Village.

PM Press was founded at the end of 2007 by a small collection of folks with decades of publishing, media, and organizing experience. PM Press co-conspirators have published and distributed hundreds of books, pamphlets, CDs, and DVDs. Members of PM have founded enduring book fairs, spearheaded victorious tenant organizing campaigns, and worked closely with bookstores, academic conferences, and even rock bands to deliver political and challenging ideas to all walks of life. We're old enough to know what we're doing and young enough to know what's at stake.

We seek to create radical and stimulating fiction and non-fiction books, pamphlets, T-shirts, visual and audio materials to entertain, educate, and inspire you. We aim to distribute these through every available channel with every available technology—whether that means you are seeing anarchist classics at our bookfair stalls; reading our latest vegan cookbook at the café; downloading geeky fiction e-books; or digging new music and timely videos from our website.

PM Press is always on the lookout for talented and skilled volunteers, artists, activists, and writers to work with. If you have a great idea for a project or can contribute in some way, please get in touch.

PM Press
PO Box 23912
Oakland, CA 94623

Friends of PM

These are indisputably momentous times—the financial system is melting down globally and the Empire is stumbling. Now more than ever there is a vital need for radical ideas.

In the eight years since its founding—and on a mere shoestring—PM Press has risen to the formidable challenge of publishing and distributing knowledge and entertainment for the struggles ahead. With hundreds of releases to date, we have published an impressive and stimulating array of literature, art, music, politics, and culture. Using every available medium, we've succeeded in connecting those hungry for ideas and information to those putting them into practice.

Friends of PM allows you to directly help impact, amplify, and revitalize the discourse and actions of radical writers, filmmakers, and artists. It provides us with a stable foundation from which we can build upon our early successes and provides a much-needed subsidy for the materials that can't necessarily pay their own way. You can help make that happen—and receive every new title automatically delivered to your door once a month—by joining as a Friend of PM Press. And, we'll throw in a free T-shirt when you sign up.

Here are your options:
- $30 a month: Get all books and pamphlets plus 50% discount on all webstore purchases
- $40 a month: Get all PM Press releases (including CDs and DVDs) plus 50% discount on all webstore purchases
- $100 a month: Superstar—Everything plus PM merchandise, free downloads, and 50% discount on all webstore purchases

For those who can't afford $30 or more a month, we're introducing Sustainer Rates at $15, $10, and $5. Sustainers get a free PM Press T-shirt and a 50% discount on all purchases from our website.

Your Visa or Mastercard will be billed once a month, until you tell us to stop. Or until our efforts succeed in bringing the revolution around. Or the financial meltdown of Capital makes plastic redundant. Whichever comes first.